GODLUST

In memory of
Henri Nouwen

Shalt thou give Law to God, shalt thou dispute
With him the points of liberty, who made
Thee what thou art, and form'd the Pow'rs of Heav'n
Such as he pleas'd, and circumscrib'd their being?
Yet by experience taught we know how good,
And of our good, and of our dignity
How provident he is, how far from thought
To make us less, bent rather to exalt
Our happy state...

Paradise Lost, Book V

GODLUST

Facing the Demonic, Embracing the Divine

Kerry Walters

Paulist Press
New York / Mahwah, N.J.

Biblical texts are cited according to the Revised Standard Version.

The Publisher gratefully acknowledges use of the following: Excerpts from *Religious Drama 2: Mystery and Morality Plays* edited by E. Martin Browne. Copyright 1977 by Peter Smith Publisher, Inc. (Gloucester, Mass.). Used with permission. Excerpts from *The Wakefield Mystery Plays* edited by Martial Rose. Copyright 1963 by Doubleday, a division of Random House. Used with permission. Excerpts from *W. H. Auden: Collected Poems* by W. H. Auden, edited by Edward Mendelson. Copyright 1940 and renewed 1968 by W. H. Auden. Reprinted by permission of Random House, Inc.

Cover design by Morris Berman Studio

Copyright © 1999 by Kerry Walters

Library of Congress Cataloging-in-Publication Data

Walters, Kerry S.
    Godlust : facing the demonic, embracing the divine / Kerry Walters.
        p.   cm.
    Includes bibliographical references.
    ISBN 0-8091-3915-4 (alk. paper)
    1. Pride and vanity. 2. Envy. 3. Herod Agrippa I, King of Judea, 10 B.C.–44 A.D. 4. Sin, Unpardonable. I. Title.
    BV4627.P7W35 1999
    241'.3—dc21   99-40429
                                                                        CIP

Published by Paulist Press
997 Macarthur Boulevard
Mahwah, New Jersey 07430

www.paulistpress.com

Printed and bound in the
United States of America

Table of Contents

Acknowledgments

I'm always amazed and humbled at the gift of friendship, and never more so than when I consider the people who graciously share their time and energy with me when I write a book. Merely mentioning their names seems small recompense, but at least it's something. This time I'm especially grateful to Karmen MacKendrick and Bruce Melim for their cheerful and insightful advice; to Ed and Cynthia Johnson for their continuing support; to my good friend Patty Bacon, who helped me through a rough time; to my editor, Kathleen Walsh, who wields her blue pencil with expertise, grace, and wit; to Kim and Jonah for enduring with good humor my authorial moodiness; and finally, to Henri Nouwen, who has taught and continues to teach me so very much. This book is a thanks-offering for his life and ministry.

Chapter One

You Will Be Like God

So boyles the fired Herod's blood-swolne brest,
...The worme of jealous envy and unrest,
To which his gnaw'd heart is the growing food.
Richard Crashaw

Dreams of the far future destiny of
man were dragging up from its
shallow and unquiet grave the old
dream of Man as God.

C. S. Lewis

The Worm in the Heart

There are few characters from the ancient Near East more unsavory than Herod the Great, tetrarch of Galilee and king of Judea. A man of ferocious temper and manic violence, Herod brutalized his subjects for forty-odd years and even slaughtered members of his own family when the rage was upon him. His fury was so murderous that the Roman emperor Augustus, himself no paragon of temperance, quipped he'd rather be Herod's pig than Herod's son. History concurs with the appraisal; for two millennia now, Herod's name has been synonymous with villainy.

King Herod is the inspiration for this book about the ways in which we humans pervert our natural desire for God. The unhappy truth is that all of us are Herods to one degree or another. True, few if any of us will match his bloodthirsty rapacity. Yet we carry within our hearts the identical worm that turned in Herod's, and our own misdeeds are of the same kind, even if not the same intensity, as his.

The worm of discontent that rotted Herod's soul and threatens ours is the lust to throw off the constraints of humanhood and become God—not, mind you, "godly" or "godlike," but *God*. Even though it's but rarely acknowledged for what it is, this obsession is always present. It insinuates itself into our everyday relationships with other people, our ways of looking at the world, and our ideas about who we are and what we want or deserve out of life. It's a poison that eventually destroys us unless we steel ourselves to admit its existence and then collaborate with divine grace to purge it from our spiritual systems. It is what blocks us from growing into a proper relationship with God and becoming the persons we are meant to be. It is the Original Sin.

This chthonic and pervasive urge to usurp God's place, this burning mania to *be* God, this worm that turns in our hearts just as surely as it twisted in Herod's, is what I call *Godlust*. Subsequent chapters examine specific ways in which Godlust corrupts our desires, intellect, and will. They also explore strategies for escaping its ensnarement and reestablishing our relationship with God. But first we need to come to a better general understanding of the worm's nature and baleful effects. And for that, we can do no better than to return to King Herod.

This Is My World!

Franco Zeffirelli's *Jesus of Nazareth* is not a particularly good film, but it does have its moments of brilliance. One of them is the scene in which an aging Herod, masterfully played by Peter Ustinov, learns that three Magi have visited Bethlehem to pay homage to an infant. Herod is perplexed. Why would these outlanders risk his anger by crossing the frontier of his kingdom without permission? What could be so important about an anonymous babe in an obscure village? And what's this mysterious star the Magi are said to have used as a beacon? In response to his questions a Temple priest reminds Herod of the ancient prophecy (Mi 5:2) that out of Bethlehem will come a ruler of Israel.

The words ignite Herod's smoldering uneasiness into hot fear and burning rage. He barks out orders for the immediate slaughter of all children in Bethlehem under the age of two. When his horrified advisors protest, the old king explodes. His face purple with fury, Herod stomps through the mausoleum-like hall of his palace shrieking at his cowering retainers.

> I'll bring down their stars! I'll snuff them out in blood! This is *my* world! I will not share it with an infant! There's no room for two kings here! You know the mark of a real king? Courage! Even in the face of Jewish prophecy! Kill! Kill! Kill them!

We live in a time when psychological explanations of human behavior have dethroned spiritual ones, and so a standard reading of Herod's outburst is to see it as the tantrum of a psychotic despot. Persons accustomed to absolute power sooner or later succumb to a galloping paranoia that brooks no challenge. At the slightest hint that their sovereignty is jeopardized they pull out the stops and explode in lunatic fury. From this perspective, Herod's reaction to the news that a rival king has been born is a predictable, even if pathological, defense reaction.

While such an interpretation isn't incorrect, it's not satisfying either. It fails to dig deeply enough. Of course Herod's outburst can be described in psychological terms, but its roots are spiritual in nature and embedded in the soul malady of Godlust. The giveaway is Herod's insistence that the world in which he dwells is *his* world, that there isn't room in *his* world for more than one center of gravity, and that he doesn't intend sharing *his* world with anyone else. Herod's ranting makes one point crystal clear: So far as he's concerned, he and he alone is the sun around which all creation spins. Any person foolish enough to interfere with his celestial primacy must be destroyed. Jewish prophecy and the Jewish God? Miraculous stars and messianic infants? Bah! Herod doesn't give a damn for any of them! The courage to smash opposition ruthlessly: This is what real lordship is all about! And *any* challenger to Herod is by definition a usurper, a second-rate wanna-be deity, because there is only one God and he is Herod.

In ages past, when the reality of spiritual maladies was taken for granted, Herod's self-divinization was easily recognized. The medieval mystery play *Herod and the Kings*, a favorite in England some six hundred years ago, makes such a diagnosis without apology or second thought. In the play a strutting Herod proudly sings his own hymn of praise:

Qui *status in* Jude *et Rex* Israel,
And the mightiest conqueror that ever walked on ground;
For I am even he that made both heaven and hell
And of my mighty power holdeth up this world round...

I am the cause of this great light and thunder:
It is through my fury that they such noise do make.
My fearful countenance the clouds doth so encumber
That oft-times for dread thereof the very earth doth
    quake...
All the world from the north to the south
I may them destroy with one word of my mouth...

To recount unto you my innumerable substance,
That were too much for any tongue to tell,
For all the whole orient is under my obedience....[1]

To the modern ear, all this sounds like the ravings of mega-lomania. But to an age innocent of psychology, Herod's self-description revealed his true spiritual colors. Omit the first-person pronoun and what's left over is an obvious listing of divine qualities. The subject of the monologue is the supreme Creator of reality ("he that made both heaven and hell"), the Sustainer of all that is (his "mighty power holdeth up this world round"), the Controller of natural phenomena ("the cause of great light and thunder"), and an entity of absolute Being ("innumerable substance") whose splendor and majesty are beyond human comprehension ("too much for any tongue to tell") and whose mighty wrath makes "the very earth" to "quake." Obviously these are all traditional descriptions of God. But the point is that Herod uses the grammatical first person; his speech is about himself:

Behold *my* countenance and *my* colour,
Brighter than the sun in the middle of the day.[2]

Herod is God, and the world illumined by his countenance is *his* world. A perfect case study, this, of the presumption that characterizes Godlust. Herod's example is well worth keeping in mind because, as I mentioned earlier, the corruption that ruined him is latent in us all. Herod's case is more advanced than ours, but the same spiritual taint flows through our bloodstream.

Desire and Lust

The soul disorder of Godlust strikes when the deepest inclination of the human heart runs amok. Put in starkest terms, the desire *for* God that lies at the core of our spiritual identities mutates into a lust *to be* God. What originally is a divinely embedded yearning that draws us toward God corrupts into an obsessive drive to usurp God's place. In the biological realm genetic mutations sometimes actually enhance the survival potential of the organisms in which they occur. But in matters of the spirit, mutations are always destructive. When God-desire rolls over into Godlust, the course of our spiritual evolution, whose proper destination is always and everywhere God, deflects into a downward spiral.

It's important at the outset to emphasize the distinction between desire and lust. Popular opinion tends to reduce desire to any psychological or sensuous itch that demands to be scratched, and lust becomes nothing more than a particularly intense desire. But the actual state of affairs is much more complicated. As its Latin root suggests, desire is the attraction to something that genuinely *fulfills* our deepest needs rather than merely *gratifies* or *satiates* our transitory wants. The aim of desire is not so much to satisfy our craving for fleetingly pleasant sensations as to awaken in us an abiding and sensitive yearning for all that we require to flourish spiritually.

The ultimate object of desire is God, the holy Source and sacred Ground of our being. Few of us immediately encounter this supremely fulfilling and hence supremely desirable Object through mystical ecstasy, but all of us are attracted by vestiges of God's Being discernible in the everyday world in which we live. These reflections, which Saint Bonaventure referred to as divine "footprints" and the contemporary thinker Peter Berger aptly calls "signals of transcendence," direct our desire toward a Reality that lies beyond but nonetheless saturates the commonplace.[3] The experience of these divine signatures triggers celebration and awed gratitude on our part. When we encounter them they call us out of ourselves, away from our usual ego absorption. They grant us a glimpse—and this is the secret of their desirability—of a depth of Being that we sense is our true home, our real medium, and the necessary condition for our completion as human beings.

Any number of seemingly ordinary experiences can serve as signals of transcendence that awaken our desire for God. Berger speaks, for example, of humor and joyful play as worldly reflections of God's perfect love and creativity. Others have suggested that experiences of hope, depth, or the future also provide opportunities for transcendent desire.[4] But from the church's very beginning, three signals of transcendence have been especially emphasized: truth, beauty, and goodness. When any of them are experienced, we catch a glimpse of their divine Source, of that Entity whom Christians believe is absolute Truth, unblemished Beauty, and supreme Goodness.[5] As Dionysius the Areopagite says, these three aspects are so interwoven in the divine essence that they are properly "names" of God, and when we think of one we necessarily call to mind the others as well.[6] A meeting with any of the worldly signals of transcendence that gesture at divine Truth, Beauty, and Goodness pulls our spiritual gaze away from self and toward that which the signals imperfectly reflect. Anyone who has experienced the awesome "Eureka!" moment of insight and self-forgetfulness (truth), lost herself in the splendor of a sunrise at sea (beauty), and given or received the gift of love (goodness), has heeded the call of transcendent desire and been vouchsafed an encounter with that resplendent Being for whom the heart yearns.

Genuine desire, then, is a longing that moves us out of ourselves toward what we spiritually need. "My soul thirsts for God, for the living God" (Ps 42). Lust, on the other hand, is an egoistic obsession that focuses exclusively on what we merely want. Its aim is immediate self-gratification, with "gratification" understood as seizure and assimilation of the lusted-for object. Its only objective is to suck whatever it craves into the self. Desire is God-referential; lust is self-referential. Desire foregoes ego absorption for the sake of an encounter with sacred Being. But lust refuses to move out of its own orbit. Its chief concern is satiation in the here-and-now, its primary impulse to extend its empire by appropriating whatever it covets. Like a rapacious protozoan, lust encircles and absorbs the objects it craves, drawing them into itself and absorbing their substance. (One is reminded here of those paintings by Dali and Picasso of nightmarish shapes with no clear-cut features save rows of sharply predatory teeth.) There is no transcendence of self in lust. On the contrary, lust transforms the self into an enormous maw that seeks to devour the entire universe.

The metaphor of devouring is crucial. Ancient peoples believed that it was possible to take on the qualities of a slain enemy by devouring his flesh. Lust operates under a similar assumption. It doesn't seek merely to *enjoy* the objects it craves. Its ultimate urge is to so utterly *possess* them that they are assimilated into the owner's identity as indissolubly as food is absorbed into tissue and cells. This is not a particularly startling claim; we see confirmations of it in the world around us all the time. The miser devours money and defines herself in terms of the amount she eats. She *is* her investment portfolio, and if she loses her fortune she loses her identity as well. The sensualist defines himself in terms of his conquests. He devours and thus absorbs the scores of anonymous bodies with which he's slept, measuring his sense of self by the number of notches on his bedpost. The power broker defines herself in terms of her ability to manipulate people and events. Deprive her of the authority on which she gorges and her self-image erodes. In a word, lust operates under the primitive assumption that you are what you eat. And lust has such a rapacious appetite that it takes the entire world as its oyster.

Ontological Anxiety

We are deiform creatures, originating from God and made in God's image. The Greek fathers frequently underscored the intimacy of this connection by saying that humans are exemplars of God just as God is the Exemplar of humans: We reflect (howsoever imperfectly) God, and God's nature in turn reflects us.

As a deiform entity our spiritual DNA is stamped with traces of the Divine that link us in a primordial, underivative way with the God whose creative love wills us into existence. Like calls to like: God within seeks to embrace God without, and we feel the tug of our connection with divine Being. But because we are creatures *like* and not *identical* to the Creator, we also feel our own incompleteness, our fundamental separateness from God. Our deiform nature underscores our distance from the ultimate Object of desire, then, even as it connects us to it—compelling us, remarks Ilias the Presbyter, "to stand midway between darkness and light."[7] Connectedness bequeaths us a great hope for the glory of ultimate reunion, an anticipation fueled by the foretastes we enjoy in our experiences of signals of transcendence such as truth, beauty, and goodness. But separateness carries with it the possibility of a fearful and forlorn alienation. As Saint Augustine observed, humans possess a bone-deep sense of lack that yearns to be filled.[8] This yearning can lead either to hopeful God-desire or a frustrated sense of incompleteness and inadequacy.

Our deiform nature necessarily swings us back and forth between these contrary responses to our incompleteness. Sometimes our lack reminds us of our connectedness to ultimate Being and we fill with joyfully expectant God-desire. But on other occasions it overwhelms us with horrible apprehension and we are paralyzed by ontological anxiety—a dread of the incompleteness of our own being. So we oscillate between these two responses, now aglow with a sense of connectedness, now burdened by a sense of separateness. This is the human condition. It is the promise but also the cross of creatures who participate in God but are not themselves God, who are beings rather than Being.

When the sense of connectedness is in the ascendancy, it nudges us to seek out the divine Being in whom we feel the promise of fulfillment. This is the essence of God-desire. But when the shadows of fear and inadequacy born from our separateness engulf us, God-desire mutates into Godlust. Our primary yearning is no longer for the Being whose fullness and splendor we sense in our transcendent moments with truth, goodness, and beauty. It detours into a blind desperation to palliate ontological anxiety by seizing for ourselves the fullness whose lack torments us. God-desire recognizes the presumptuous impossibility of such self-divinization and is content to flow toward the Fountainhead with whom its deiformity connects it. Godlust, driven to frenzy by its overwhelming sense of deprivation, can neither admit nor tolerate the impossibility of self-divinization. So instead of flowing outside itself and giving itself over to what will complete it, it attempts to seize and absorb what it covets. Nothing short of *becoming* the Fountainhead will do.

Existential Envy

Another way to grasp the mutation of God-desire into God-lust is to see it as the consequence of a spiritual phenomenon the German philosopher Max Scheler called "existential envy."

Garden variety envy is a common psychological reaction that's bred, Scheler says, from "a feeling of impotence which we experience when another person owns a good we covet."[9] My neighbor buys a winning lottery ticket and I envy her luck. My fellow office worker is given the promotion I want and I envy her success. I envy the movie star his good looks and the genius her brains. In all these instances, the target of my envy is a quality or object I crave but that others possess. But envy of this kind generally is short-lived. Either I stew for a while in self-pitying resentment until my jealousy fades away; or I compensate for my felt lack—what Scheler refers to as "impotence"—by achieving victories in other arenas; or I convince myself that I never really wanted the unattainable object of envy in the first place (a rationalization perfectly illustrated, by the way, in Aesop's fable about the fox and the grapes).

But the spiritual condition of existential envy is quite distinct from the run-of-the-mill variety we so frequently experience. Both its target and intensity are different. When we slip into existential envy, our jealousy is directed not at a quality or object owned by another, but rather at that person's *very existence*. I go beyond craving the movie star's good looks. Instead, I long to *be* the movie star himself. I no longer envy my neighbor her good fortune. Now I envy her sheer *existence* as a person-with-a-winning-lottery-ticket. Existential envy lusts to exchange being with the person whom it targets. This craving for the other's identity is nicely captured in commonplace expressions like "I wish I was Cindy Crawford!" or "Boy, if only I could trade places with Donald Trump!"

The second distinctive feature of existential envy is that its intensity escalates rather than diminishes with time. Existential envy isn't merely a transitory irritation, but rather an urgent, obsessive want that sinks into the soul and consumes it with a flaming sense of resentful deprivation. The envied person is transformed into a hostile and hated "Other" whose will opposes mine.[10] She becomes the cause of my incompleteness because she is what I want to be but cannot. As long as she exists I'm forever inadequate, and my bitterness continuously whispers: "I can forgive everything, but not that you are—that you are *what* you are—that I am not what you are—indeed that I am not *you*."[11] There's no way out except for me somehow to become her, and that of course entails her destruction. Since it's not a quality or object of hers for which I lust, I can't slack my craving by taking any *thing* away from her. No, what I covet is her very being, and to achieve that I must devour *her*.

The Godluster suffers from hypertrophic existential envy, because the object of his lustful jealousy is God rather than another person. The weight of his ontological anxiety burdens him with such a pervasive sense of his own incompleteness that God, who possesses the plenitude he lacks and covets, becomes an object of resentment rather than adoration, the Other who mocks and jeers at his impotence. God has the fullness the Godluster craves; it is divine existence itself that he envies. Very well, then: He will destroy God and take for his own God's plenitude. He will devour God and thereby become God.

Eating God

When we are suffused with a joyful sense of our deiformic connectedness, we *partake* of God. We recognize that our hunger can be assuaged by only one Food, and we gratefully come to the banquet prepared for us, focusing not on our appetites but on the splendor of the repast. This movement away from self and toward divine nourishment is epitomized in the Eucharist, where we humbly accept the sacrificial gift God makes of himself to us and rejoice in our dependency on it.[12]

But when the burden of our separateness collapses celebratory desire into ontological anxiety and existential envy, we so obsessively fixate on our hunger that we lust to *devour* rather than to partake of God. Along with the ancients who believed they could acquire the physical and moral strength of heroes by eating their flesh, we strive to compensate for our sensed lack by ingesting the fullness that properly belongs only to God and that we so resentfully covet. Like the Israelites in the wilderness, we rebelliously test God "by demanding the food [we] crave" (Ps 78:18; cf. Nm 11:4–20).

That food is divine strength and knowledge and power. We wish to spew out our emptiness and stuff ourselves with God's plenitude. We aim to be the creative Source rather than the "mere" recipients of signals of transcendence that point to Truth, Beauty, and Goodness.

Most of us, of course, aren't consciously aware of what we're up to when we try to eat and thereby become God. Our ancestors were more forthright. The Aztecs devoured their great god Huitzilopochtli twice a year at the solstices in order to absorb his divinity. The ceremony was called *teoqualo*, "god is eaten." Analogous practices were common among Mexico's Huichol tribe, the Ainu of Japan, and the Thompson Indians of the Pacific Northwest.[13] But for those of us in the late twentieth century who fancy ourselves "civilized," such ritualism reeks of superstition and savagery.

Our present-day theophagy is much more urbane. We tell ourselves that we are the measure of all things, that our intellects are supreme, that we are autonomous creatures in control of our own destinies, that we possess the emotional sophistication and moral wisdom to transform the world into a utopian paradise. And the way in which we take on these divine attributes is through turning God into an "absent referent."

The theologian and animal rights activist Carol Adams discusses the notion of absent referencing in connection with meat eating. She says that we transform an animal into an absent referent when we refuse to acknowledge qualities in it that show it to be a living, sentient creature rather than a mere food source. The transformation centers around a process of renaming and reconceptualization that conveniently distances us ever farther from the real animal: "this is a cow" becomes "this is beef"—"this is beefsteak"—"this is

steak"—"this is meat"—"this is food." In making the defini-
tional leap from "cow" to "food," we transform the animal into
an absent referent. What remains is the abstract concept of
"food." What's been made absent is the actual animal from
whom the food came. So now we can enjoy our "food" protected from the ugly truth that it's the cruelly slaughtered
flesh of a once-living being.[14]

Godlusters too squeamish to admit their God-eating insu-
late themselves in almost the same way animal eaters do.
Like their carnivorous brethren, they engage in the subterfuge
of absent referencing. It's just that in their case, the reference
made absent is God.

When we transform God into an absent referent, we abstract
away qualities that traditionally have been viewed as properly
divine—absolute Truth, ultimate Beauty, and supreme Goodness—and ascribe them to humans. This transfer is the source
of the conviction that humans are the measure of all things. The
devolution goes something like this: "God is Truth (Beauty/
Goodness)" becomes "Truth (Beauty/Goodness) is a quality of
God"—"Truth (Beauty/Goodness) is a Godly quality"—"Truth
(Beauty/Goodness) is a quality that makes humans God." That
to which the words *truth*, *beauty*, and *goodness* originally
referred—God—is made absent. All that remains is the
detached divine quality, and humans now possess it.

That this transfer of divine qualities to humans is one of the
ways we go about eating God is evidenced in the interpretations
of religious belief offered by Ludwig Feuerbach in the early
nineteenth century and Sigmund Freud in the twentieth. Both
men argued that God is nothing more than a human invention,
a projection of idealized human qualities such as truth, goodness, beauty, power, and so on. Peel away these qualities from
"God" and return them to their rightful bearers—humans—and

the notion of "God" is revealed for what it is: nothing, an absence. In defending this argument, both Feuerbach and Freud anticipated the strategy of absent-referencing God. Neither of them, of course, thought of it as presumptuous Godlust. Instead, they saw it as a means by which humans could reassert their sovereignty over themselves and the world, and dressed it with the laudatory label of "humanism." But for all that, it is a way of devouring God in order to take God's place.[15]

The truth of the matter is this: Try as we may to sanitize our God-eating through absent referencing, we "humanists" have savagely tracked down, captured, slain, carved up, and eaten the deity. God is now within us, which is to say that we now *are* God. Unlike his more delicate fellow travelers, the nineteenth-century God-eater Max Stirner scorned to shilly-shally around the issue with anthropological or psychological jargon. "If you *devour the sacred*," he triumphantly promised, "you have made it your own! Digest the sacramental wafer, and you are rid of it!"[16]

As we've seen, the God-eating impulse so honestly advocated by Stirner stems from a rebellious anxiety over one's lack of plenitude: Fill up on God and one no longer has anything to fear or envy. Lust for any object is ultimately traceable to this same anxiety. The miser's lust for money, the sensualist's obsession with sexual conquest, the power broker's incessant drive to be in command: What else are these but instinctual attempts at self-divinization? Money, sexual manipulation, and power bestow at least an illusion of the fullness we so crave. We want them not for their own sake, but because we lust to be God. Covetousness in any guise, accordingly, reflects the chthonic obsession to remake our being into Being by eating God. As Augustine noted, "...lust is dominant in every kind of evildoing."[17] The worm ever turns,

Original Sin ever reasserts itself, even if we refuse to acknowledge its reality.

The Original Sin

Godlust first and foremost is rebellion against God. In tracing this urge to devour God to ontological anxiety, I don't mean to psychologize it and thus downplay its sinful nature. Granted, as deiform beings all of us necessarily oscillate between moments of connected desire and separated forlornness. Christian tradition has always recognized the inevitability of periodic dark nights of the soul, and the troughs all of us encounter in our personal faith journeys unpleasantly verify the point. But even though we can't avoid such bleak interludes, we are responsible for how we respond to them. We can choose to endure and even learn from them, possessing our souls in patience as best we can until they pass, trusting that the alienated sense of separateness that crushes us is but the shadow side of our more fundamental connectedness. Such endurance, as we'll see in subsequent chapters, calls for a relinquishment of one's egoistic urges toward self-control and ego gratification, and this is a free act of the will. Or we can succumb to anxiety and envy, allowing them to twist our innate desire for God into a chronic state of proud and rebellious Godlust. This too is a freely willed choice. The fact that Godlust is one possible response to the deiformic separateness from God that is our lot may explain its origin. But it cannot mitigate its sinfulness.

The Bible is an epic telling of the oscillation that sometimes swings us out of ourselves into God-desire and at other times thrusts us back onto ourselves in Godlust. There's high drama here: The worm in the heart locked in spiritual struggle with God and humans, the constant human temptation to break under the pain of separateness pitted against the divine invitation to partake rather than devour. Each moral or spiritual triumph recorded in scripture is ultimately a victory over the mania to be God.

Since Godlust is the invidious source from which all other lusts spring, and since it's also the most fundamental kind of rebellion against God, it is *the* Original Sin. The prophet Isaiah recognized as much when he rebuked the presumptuousness of kings and commoners alike:

> You have said in your heart,
> "I will ascend to heaven;
> above the stars of god
> I will set my throne on high;
> I will sit on the mount of assembly in the far north;
> I will ascend above the heights of the clouds,
> I will make myself like the Most High." (14:13–14)

The lust to be "like the Most High," which Isaiah deplores as humankind's rock-bottom temptation, is an obvious reference to the story of Adam and Eve's ancient fall in the Garden of Eden. There the Evil One hissed into the primordial couple's ears the promise that they could "be like God," the Most High, if they but willed it (Gn 3:5). Adam and Eve knew themselves to be incomplete, dependent upon Yahweh for their being. (In this regard, it's interesting to note that *Yahweh* seems to be derived from the Hebrew *hawah*, "to be." Thus God is the Being that grounds all being.[18]) True, they had been given much; as Milton put it, they were "Lords declar'd of all in Earth or Air."[19] But what good is dominion over earth and air when one can't likewise command heaven? Without that, nothing is secure; everything can be lost. If one is not God, one is nothing. And if one is nothing, existence is too perilous to be endured.

The Tempter knew all too well the ache of deiformic separateness. After all, he had succumbed to an angelic version of Godlust himself, thereby losing Paradise (cf. 2 Pt 2:4). So (again in Milton's words) he coiled himself around the Edenic tree, pretended to eat its fruit, and attacked Eve at her most vulnerable spot:

> O Sacred, Wise, and Wisdom-giving Plant,
> Mother of Science, Now I feel thy Power
> Within me clear, not only to discern
> Things in their Causes, but to trace the ways
> Of highest Agents deem'd however wise.
> Queen of this Universe, do not believe
> Those rigid threats of Death; ye shall not Die:
> How should ye? by the Fruit? it gives you Life....[20]

It's significant that the Old Testament links the entry of sin into the world with the act of eating. The fruit devoured by Adam and Eve is a metaphor for God's essence. It contains the promise of divine knowledge and hence divine power ("Wisdom-giving Plant, Mother of Science"), and in consuming it the primordial couple in effect consume God. *You will be like God*: The moment this desperate strategy for overcoming ontological anxiety is seized, the worm burrows deep into the human heart and begins its relentless gnawing.

The Original Sin symbolized by Adam and Eve's craving for the forbidden fruit resurfaces time and again throughout the Hebrew scriptures. The construction of the tower at Babel, a spire intended to breach heaven for an all-out invasion so that humans could "make a name" for themselves (Gn 11:4); Pharaoh's arrogant "Who is the Lord, that I"—that is, a God in my *own* right—"should heed his voice?" (Ex 5:2); the abuse of power and assumption of divine prerogative exercised by the kings of Judea and Israel, including even David, God's anointed (e.g., 2 Sm 11); the self-worship of the privileged elite condemned by prophets such as Amos and Joel: All of these are stories which chronicle the pervasiveness of God-lust. God knew what he was about in decreeing that the first commandment would be "You shall have no other gods before me" (Ex 20:3). This is the prime injunction, because self-divinization is the Original Sin from which flow all other offenses prohibited by subsequent commandments.

The New Testament's continuation of the saga of humanity's spiritual evolution also takes the struggle with the Original Sin of Godlust as its centerpiece. The crucial difference of course is that the obsession to devour God is foresworn by the new Adam, Jesus the Christ. This doesn't mean that the worm is plucked from the human heart; the temptation to eat God remains so long as humans feel the ache of ontological anxiety, and the latter is always a possibility for deiform creatures. But the new Adam's triumph over Godlust guarantees that it *is* surmountable.

The centrality of Godlust in the New Testament is demonstrated by the fact that both the Christian and Hebrew scriptures take it for a thematic overture. In the Old Testament, the story of Edenic Godlust was the opening chapter in the history of humanity; Christian scripture begins the *new* history of humanity with the story of Jesus' wilderness temptations to Godlust.

When God-in-Jesus deigned to pitch his tent among us in order to give the human race a second chance, he became fully human, relinquishing divine plenitude for mortal incompleteness. As such, he became subject to the same ontological anxiety that haunts all persons. Scripture relates at least

three occasions when Jesus despaired over his sense of separateness: the struggle in the wilderness (Mt 4:1–22; Mk
1:12–13; Lk 4:1–13), the horrible night at Gethsemane (Mt
26:36–44; Mk 14:32–40; Lk 22:40–44), and the great cry of des-
olation from the cross (Mt 27:46; Mk 15:34). The most significant of these three is the wilderness struggle, providing as it
does the most obvious allusion to Godlust.

We are told that during the forty days of solitary soul-
searching in the desert, preceding his public ministry, Jesus
was tested in three ways. The first was to satisfy his hunger by
magically transforming stones into bread; the second was to
defy natural law by throwing himself off a precipice without
harm to life or limb; and the third was to take absolute control of peoples and nations. The allure of the Evil One's three
gifts was identical to that which seduced Adam and Eve: *You
will be like God.* Only God is powerful enough to gratify his every
wish; only God can circumvent natural law; and only God
exercises supreme sovereignty over the world. Jesus went into
the wilderness to grow in his relationship with God, but the
worm in the heart sought to mutate his God-desire into Godlust. When Satan volunteered to help Jesus transform stone
into bread, the actual repast he offered was God.

Jesus successfully resisted the urge to devour God. His
final word to Satan, that there is already a God worthy of wor-
ship and allegiance (Mt 4:10), was a paraphrase of the first
commandment's warning against self-divinization. At that
moment Jesus proved that the ontological anxiety and existential envy provoked by separateness aren't as strong as the
joyful God-desire inspired by connectedness, and thereby
showed the way through and beyond Original Sin.

But scripture attests to the fact that even though Jesus
refused to allow ontological anxiety to enslave his spirit,

humans both then and now are still gnawed by it. The rest of the New Testament is a warning of how Godlust continues to insinuate itself into the heart and a promise that Christ's victory over it offers us a way out as well. We see the urge to devour God emerge even in the apostles themselves: During Jesus' earthly ministry James and John and Peter explicitly hope their discipleship will bring them power and dominion over the world (Mt 19:27; 20:20–23; Mk 10:35–40), and none of the apostles seem to appreciate until after the resurrection that the true goals of a follower of Christ are love and service rather than kingship (e.g., Lk 22:24; Jn 13:2–9). Simon Magus, a would-be apostle, petitions Christ's followers to teach him words of power so that he might command reality and become a God (Acts 8:18–19). Paul continuously admonishes his correspondents to resist Godlust by renouncing their holier-than-thou judgmentalism as well as their craving of pleasures and worldly advancement (e.g., Rom 14:4–14; 1 Cor 6:13–15; 10:24; 2 Cor 12:9–10; Eph 5; Phil 2:3–4). And Christian eschatology teaches that Godlust's final and most furious assault will be the appearance of the Antichrist in the endtime (2 Thes 2:8; 2 Cor 6:15; Rev 20:8). The absolute power of Godlust to enslave may have been broken by Jesus' victory, but each person is still called upon to collaborate in the struggle against it.

The Devouring God

Our knowledge of God is always limited. How could it be otherwise with finite creatures such as ourselves? A sponge cannot hope to soak up the ocean. But Godlust adds distortion to limitation. Even as it perverts our innate inclination toward God, it also corrupts our understanding of what it means to be God. The divine being God-eaters crave to be is a

caricature of the one true God. It is God made in their rapacious and insecure image. In devouring God, they become
Gods-who-devour. They become Molochs.

Moloch is the corrupt pagan deity whose insatiable appetite
demanded children as burnt offerings (Lv 18:21; 20:2–5; 2 Kgs
23:10; Jer 32:35). Isaiah (30:33) tells us that his name, appropri-
ately, is a corruption of the Hebrew word (*melech*) for "king." A
genuine king does not consume his own people, just as a genuine God does not hunger for human sacrifice: "I desire steadfast love...rather than burnt offerings" (Hos 6:6).

But this is a point that eludes the God-eater. His voracious
appetite to escape his anxious sense of inadequacy not only
drives him to devour God; it also inexorably pushes him to
consume the universe as well. His notion of what it means to
be God is a tribalistic one: God is a tyrannical chieftain, an
oriental satrap whose will is law. The God-who-devours
insists that he and he alone decides what's true and false. The
God-who-devours exercises arbitrary control and dominion
over the earth and the heavens. The God-who-devours
strong-arms people to do his bidding. The devouring God, in
short, sucks all creation into his belly. Like Herod, the world
is his to do with what he will. This, so the Godluster concludes, is the obvious prerogative of a divine Being.

Where the aspiring God-who-devours goes wrong, however, is in supposing that the consumption of reality will
assuage his ontological anxiety. On the contrary, such gorging
only exacerbates his oppressive sense of incompleteness.
There are two reasons for this.

In the first place, the simple fact is that the Godluster can
never succeed in devouring the entire universe. Despite his
strutting, he remains after all a limited, finite, and rather
pathetic creature. As Kierkegaard observed, a human may

succeed in becoming "greater, greater, greatest, exceedingly and astonishingly the greatest man that ever lived"—but never God.[21] Try as he might, the planets will not dance to his tune, people will resist his manipulations, and truth will defy his attempts to define and monopolize it. All his projects will finally collapse in frustrated abortion, and his tormented sense of deprivation will only increase.

Secondly, the Godluster's efforts to assume divinity for himself necessarily drive him from the true God's presence, making his forlornness even more intolerable. Sin is the refusal to accept God's invitation to walk in God's ways, and its consequences are truly hellish: a self-imposed banishment from God. Rebellion against God and the ensuing horror of exile both reach their apex in Godlust. By refusing to embrace his deiform connectedness with the divine, the Godluster drives himself further and further into an alien land of rock and shadow. Like his ancestor Cain, the weight of his loneliness and shame is too great to bear. But also like Cain, the Godluster disdains to seek redemption because doing so is an admission of weakness, and a god is not weak. Moloch's conceit of self-sufficiency is as infinite as his appetite. He will not admit the possibility that he's always ravenous because there's something fundamentally diseased about his appetite. Instead, he concludes that he simply hasn't eaten enough.

Deification and Demonization

Just as Godlust is a perversion of God-desire, so its aim of self-divinization is a perversion of the human soul's true goal. Our proper end is not to *be God* but to *become Godlike* by rejoining the eternal and loving Source whence we came and for which our hearts ache: "You shall become holy; for I the Lord your

God am holy" (Lv 19:2). The Greek fathers called this spiritual transformation *theopoiesis* or "deification." Saint Maximos the Confessor describes it as the "inexpressible interpenetration" of the yearning soul with that for which it yearns.

> Through that interpenetration the believer finally returns to his origin. This return is the fulfillment of desire. Fulfillment of desire is ever-active repose in the object of desire. Such repose is eternal uninterrupted enjoyment of this object. Enjoyment of this kind entails participation in supranatural divine realities. This participation consists in *the participant becoming like that in which he participates*. Such likeness involves, so far as this is possible, an identity with respect to energy between the participant and that in which he participates by virtue of the likeness.[22]

What's the nature of this ultimate Object of desire in whom the deified soul participates in "ever-active repose"? The pre-Christian Plato said it well:

> Let me tell you then why the creator made this world.... He was good, and the good can never have any jealousy of anything. And being free from jealousy, he desired that all things should be as like himself as they could be. This is in the truest sense the origin of creation and of the world....God desired that all things should be good and nothing bad, so far as this was attainable.[23]

Contrary to the Moloch-like divinity on which the Godluster sets his sights, the true God is not a devourer. The true God sacrifices rather than takes, nurtures rather than enslaves, fulfills rather than deplenishes, loves rather than manipulates. The true God is not a jealous tyrant who struts his authority and hysterically crushes opposition. Instead, he empties himself for the good of humankind and all creation, willing to endure the pain of unrequited love and even outright hatred in order to coax us out of our envious darkness and into the light. As Saint Mark the Ascetic wrote, "The Logos became man, so that man might become Logos. Being rich, He became poor for our sakes, so that through His poverty we might become rich. In His great love for man He became like us, so that through every virtue we might become like Him."[24]

This is true Godhood. This is what being God is all about. Poor Herod was as wrong as he could be. Genuine Lordship isn't about seizure and possession, but about loving sacrifice. It isn't a ravenous intaking so much as a beneficent outpouring. We grow into God's likeness—we advance along the path of deification—to the degree that we resist the temptation of Original Sin by imitating the divine emptying. This implies, as John Meyendorff says, a dynamic, open, and purposeful decision on our part to shed self and direct our energies in love toward God and our fellows.[25] We lose to gain; in dying we live.

Godlust's obsession with self-divinization goes in the opposite direction. It leads to death rather than life—death of the soul and desiccation of the desire for God that animates the soul. Self-divinization is actually demonization. God is the unconditioned Being out of whom flows meaning and truth, beauty and holiness, goodness and love. As such, to invoke Paul Tillich's expression, God and God alone is worthy of our "ultimate concern." But the identifying mark of demonization is its attempt to bestow divine absoluteness on a finite object and spotlight it as the object of ultimate concern.[26] In the case of Godlust, that object is the self. In a perverse way, the God-eater's ultimate concern *is* God; it's just that the "God" with whom he's ultimately concerned is himself.

In a set of posthumously published lectures, Daniel Day Williams brilliantly discussed this demonic urge to absolutize the finite and discovered in it no fewer than five essential characteristics. Four of them are especially pertinent here. Williams concluded that the demonic attracts because it is *fascinating*: It "quickens interest and excitement [and] releases our passionate energies." The fascination of the demonic is at least partly accounted for by the fact that it is *perceived as revelatory*: It is experienced as a "disclosure of depth," of "power in the depth of things." But the revelation is dangerous, because the demonic always *distorts*: "...the demonic gains its power to shape, exploit, and ultimately destroy our personal being by causing us to see falsely." Moreover, the demonic is also *aggrandizing*, demanding more and more: It is "swollen with the lust for power. Its craving is insatiable because it feeds upon its power of domination."[27]

Williams's description of the demonic obviously applies to the chthonic urge to be God. Godlust by its very nature is aggrandizing; it prompts the Godluster to eat the entire universe and take control of it. It is even more apparently a distortion: The Godluster is not and cannot be God. But in spite of the inevitability of failure (which surely even the Godluster must at some deep level sense), he perseveres. The ambition to be God, as Williams says, quickens the pulse. We are thrilled and invigorated by even our paltry pursuits of wealth and prestige. How much more exhilarating is the decision to go for the golden ring, the whole enchilada—to become God! And when we do begin to walk down the road that so allured Herod, we fancy that great reservoirs of personal will power and wisdom and fortitude and goodness are progressively revealed to us. We flex our muscles and their strength surprises us. We realize, *we know*, that we have inside us the stuff to be God, that we can free ourselves from our mortal limitations and assume our rightful place at the center of things. Along with the contemporary philosopher E. D. Klemke, we are gladdened by the death of God, "for thereby is man all the more glorious."[28]

But this is all delusion. When demonic Godlust takes hold of us we are not liberated. Instead, Godlust so hideously perverts our deiformic nature that we are plunged "from deep to deeper" into an "Abyss of fears."[29] The worm ravishes the heart until it reduces it to a putrid horror pulsating with hatred and agony and despair. The corruption that overtook the dying Herod's physical frame—"unbearable itching, constant pains in the lower bowel, swellings on the feet as in dropsy, inflammation of the abdomen, and mortification of the genitals, producing worms as well as difficulty in breathing, and spasms in all his limbs"[30]—is but an outward sign of the spiritual decay wrought by his demonic Godlust. It is also a sign for us, a reminder of the momentous stakes in the choice between deification or demonization that faces each of us today even as it confronted Herod two millennia ago.

The God-Eater's Menu

The chapters that follow explore more fully the dynamics of that choice by focusing on three basic ways in which the ontological anxiety and existential envy born from our separateness drive us in the demonic direction of self-divinization. But they also prescribe antidotes to the spiritual poison of Godlust, each of which centers around the act of opening oneself to grace. Only grace is capable of breaking the power of the demonic; only in following its lead can we hope to cooperate in our salvation.

The three fundamental ways in which we contemporary God-eaters strive to seize divine Essence and make it our own revolve around our responses to the signals of transcendence of worldly truth, beauty, and goodness. We've seen that God-desire can be awakened and nurtured by the revelation of holy Being given in the experiences of these three divine "names." The soul on its way to deification celebrates such moments and embraces them as verifications of its connectedness to God. But the soul tortured by its oppressive sense of separateness, and hence intent on demonic self-divinization, seeks to devour rather than embrace God's Truth, Beauty, and Goodness. Eat the qualities of God and become God: This is the logic of Original Sin.

Truth-Eating. When the Godluster tries to devour Truth, he takes himself as the originator and final arbiter of truth and meaning in the world. This perverse pretension to omniscience, which today usually falls under the philosophical rubrics of "subjectivism" or "relativism," denies both objective and transcendent ground to truth and instead views it as nothing more than human invention. Such a repudiation of divine Truth reduces God to the status of an absent referent. The notion of truth remains, but now that it has been severed from God it relocates to humans—which of course bestows divinity on them.

Chapter 2 explores the nature of truth-eating by scrutinizing the influential efforts of Friedrich Nietzsche and the contemporary philosopher Richard Rorty to reduce truth to subjective interpretation and linguistic convention. As an alternative to their reduction of truth, this chapter offers the New Testament's insight into truth as *aletheia*, or unconcealment of the Real. On this reading, truth is not something we cause to be so much as a revelatory event that happens to us and thereby changes our very being. The breaking-forth of *aletheia* is ultimately initiated by God, since at its core all alethic events are divine self-disclosures. Taking a cue from Ignatius of Loyola's notion of *indiferençia*, chapter 2 argues that the cultivation of alert expectancy on our parts—an expectancy that is simultaneously a detachment from self and an attentiveness to divine presence—prepares us for receiving God's unconcealment, God's Truth.

Beauty-Eating. In devouring beauty, the Godluster tries to strip the physical realm of its beauty—a transitory and reflected beauty that points to the existence of divine and eternal Beauty. The apparent intention is to relocate divine Beauty to the self by turning God into an absent referent. Beauty, like truth, becomes an exclusively human invention, solely in the "eye of the beholder." But more fundamentally, the beauty-eater's gobbling up of beauty aims to eliminate all traces of God from nature in order to transform it into a spiritless, inert repository of raw material ripe for seizure, conquest, and absolute mastery.

This conceit of omnipotence, which typically defends itself by instrumentalist appeals to science and technology, is the focus of chapter 3. We'll examine Martin Heidegger's analysis of the perversity of beauty-eating's efforts to denude nature of God and thereby reduce the *kosmos* (the Greek word for "ornament") to a merely physical cosmos. The American theologian Jonathan Edwards and the British poet Gerard Manley Hopkins will show us the way to give up the urge to devour beauty and replace it with wonderment and joy. The world is shot through with the holy splendor of divine Beauty's presence. When we ignore it in order to fixate on the vain enterprise of conquering nature, we condemn ourselves to a barren landscape that holds no possibility of transcendence. But when we harken to the call (*kaleo*) of divine Beauty (*kalon*) embedded in nature, we return to the path of eventual deification.

Good-Eating. The final way Godlusters strive for self-divinization is in many respects the most complicated. It is the attempt to eat divine Goodness, thereby absenting God in order to make human will the sole source of the Good. The church fathers frequently pointed out that one of the most insidious ways humans go wrong is in trying to do good. Chapter 4 recasts this claim by demonstrating that the root of the problem lies not in trying to *do* good but in the self-divinizing attempt to *be* Goodness—in other words, in assuming for the self the quality of omnibenevolence.

When the Godluster devours goodness, he bestows upon himself the divine wisdom to define value and hence regulate and judge human behavior. Søren Kierkegaard argued that sometimes God suspends fidelity to the *ethical* in order to further the *Good*. When the Godluster takes for himself the prerogative of divine Goodness, he assumes the same privilege and "altruistically" overrides respect for freedom and personhood by forcing conformity to the values his will has absolutized and which he thinks will bring about utopia. But his reformist zeal, idealistic as it may seem, inevitably is an expression of his urge to exercise absolute sovereignty over people. The God-who-devours has already eaten truth and beauty; now, in order to "reform" individuals and society, he consumes the human spirit.

As an alternative to the arrogant and destructive "altruism" of the good-eater, chapter 4 offers a vision of the Good based not on the ego-generated ideals of power and perfection but rather on an imitation of God's self-emptying Love. The goal is not to force a utopian society. Instead, the aim is to nurture a community of persons who imitate God's parenting, spousal, and shepherding Love. Genuine goodness depends upon discerning the presence of Christ in others and responding to that presence in poverty of spirit and with generosity and passion. Chapter 4 draws on scriptural insights as well as on Dorothy Day and Frederick Buechner to explore ways to relinquish good-eating for the sake of following the lead of divine Love/Goodness.

Finally, we return in a brief conclusion to the distinction, introduced in this chapter, between partaking of God and devouring God. Gorging on Truth, Beauty, and Goodness is a perversion of our natural appetite or desire for God. As a consequence, the food we demand to satisfy Godlust's hunger destroys rather than sustains us, stuffing us with rust and ashes and so utterly sapping us of what Georges Bernanos calls our "virility" that we spiritually starve to death. But when with God's grace we discipline our unnatural appetite long enough to partake of the living Bread we truly need, we feast *with* and not *on* God in such a way that the divine interpenetration Saint Maximos says is the culmination of the spiritual journey is reached. In the conclusion, we'll explore more fully what it means to partake of the soul food offered us by God.

Future chapters will reveal a logic to Godlust that bestows a certain coherency, even though a demonic one, on truth-, beauty-, and good-eating. As we've already seen, they all share a common center of gravity—the self's incessant drive to become master of the universe—and this center causes them to converge in ways that are sometimes obvious and at other times subtle. Truth-eating's insistence on the supremacy of subjectivity prepares the way for beauty-eating's violent redefinition of *kosmos* as cosmos. Moreover, the same will to conquer characteristic of beauty-eating's assault on nature reasserts itself in good-eating's utopian drive to force out "imperfections" in both individuals and society. Each of the ways we go about devouring God are inseparably linked with and complement one another.

But there's also a logic appropriate to the soul's cooperation with God in its ascent to deification. The center of gravity here, of course, is self-emptying rather than self-aggrandizement, and this core likewise bestows a coherency on God-desire's alternatives to truth-, beauty-, and good-eating. When we resist the temptation to appropriate truth and instead open ourselves up in alert readiness to the experience of *aletheia*, we also nurture that egoless wonderment that makes us receptive to divine Beauty. Moreover, the selflessness we cultivate for the sake of Truth and Beauty in turn readies us for the loving service that is a true reflection and celebration of divine Goodness. The logic of grace lifts us upward toward radiance, just as the logic of Godlust hurtles us from deep to deeper. Light or darkness, as Ilias the Presbyter said, are the two great possibilities offered us by our deiform nature.

A final word. In tracing the strategies with which the modern Godluster seeks to absent God and assume divinity, I've focused on the ways *some* philosophers eat Truth (chapter 1), *some* scientists and technologists eat Beauty (chapter 2), and *some* reformers eat the Good (chapter 3). The Tempter is nothing if not opportunistic, and takes advantage of any number of human endeavors to pervert God-desire. Consequently, even the best-intentioned of philosophers, scientists, and reformers are potential raw material for the demon's purposes. But to say this is a far cry from claiming that philosophy, science and technology, or social reformism are inherently or inevitably vehicles of Godlust. When misused, each can throw up smoke screens for the sinful usurpation of divine prerogative. But when undertaken properly, each can also collaborate in the building of God's kingdom and the deification of the human soul. As Augustine wisely observed, "...some men make evil use of these things...; but the man who uses these rightly proves that they are indeed good."[31]

Chapter Two

Godlust and Truth

Jesus then said to the Jews who had believed in him, "If you continue in my word, you are truly my disciples, and you will know the truth, and the truth will make you free."

John 8:31

If this be truth, then I despair, I am undone!

Herod

Let None Speak!

Secular common sense and Christian belief alike accept the notion that truth is independent of individual will or opinion. The secular temperament grounds truth in the existence of an objective world of "factual" things and relations. We know and speak truth to the degree that our ideas and utterances correspond to this objective world. Christian belief, while not rejecting the secular understanding of truth, adds that in a deeper sense every experience of truth also reflects the eternal and unchanging God who is "the way, the *truth*, and the life" (Jn 14:6). Truth isn't just an intellectual correspondence between our perceptions and ideas about the world and the way the world is actually configured. More significantly, as we saw in the last chapter, truth is a signal of transcendence that calls us forth out of the here-and-now into the presence of Truth itself, God. To this way of thinking, truth is something that *happens* to us rather than something we passively stumble across, and it always exceeds our ability to fathom it. As such, we can never possess or own it. Moreover, when truth in this deep sense overtakes us, the consequences are not exclusively nor even primarily intellectual. Instead, our entire being is transfigured and we "live according to the truth" (cf. 1 Jn 1:6).

In either case, secular or Christian, truth is viewed as involving something "out there" rather than being a purely subjective invention or human conceit. Both the secularist and the Christian acknowledge that a complete grasp of the truth is an impossibility for any single person, and that personal limitations and prejudice necessarily distort to one extent or another our perception of it. Both likewise agree that humans frequently confuse what they want to be true with what actually is true. But these are qualifications rather than repudiations of the conviction that truth is grounded in something that exists independently of us and would continue to exist even if no humans were around to experience it.

The Godluster can't abide the traditional understanding of truth in either its secular or Christian form. If truth exists independently of his intellect or will, if it remains what it is

regardless of whether or not he experiences it or wants to accept it, then it seriously challenges his obsession to position himself at the center of reality. The Godluster can tolerate no truth that stands over and against his own will and desire because its sheer existence painfully reminds him of the anxious sense of ontological inadequacy he so longs to escape. As an aspiring deity, he and he alone must be truth's source, he and he alone in control of it. This is the function—this is the *right*—of God. Nothing less is acceptable.

The upshot is that the Godluster's need to usurp divine Being necessarily goads him to seize and absorb truth as well. If God is Truth, those who would devour God in order to be God must likewise devour Truth. Since the Godluster aims to *become* and hence determine Truth, any opinion or interpretation that refuses to conform to his own will must be rejected as presumptuous error. It's useless to try to persuade him with "facts." What does a God care for such petty things? Facts are what finite and timid beings clutch when they're confused or cornered. But a God is never at a loss. His knowledge of the universe is always perfect, always transcends the pathetic facts to which bumbling mortals cling. A God ever has the last word. This too is the function—the *right*—of God.

We can turn once more to the unhappy example of King Herod to illustrate Godlust's drive to devour Truth. Over his forty-year reign, Herod grew accustomed to laying down the law about what was true and what was false. His will was the final arbiter of which ideas were correct or incorrect, what meaning events held, which judgments were trustworthy. His interpretations alone were accurate, his verdicts the only reliable standards. Facts were of interest to him if they fed into what he omnisciently knew to be the case; in all other instances they were rejected as distortions or willful misrepresentations. To disagree or contradict his truth-defining decrees once he'd made up his mind was to court disaster. Such was the cost of contravening truth. As Herod warns his subjects in the medieval Wakefield mystery play,

> Peace, I bid, both far and near,
> Let none speak when I appear:
> Who moves his lips while I am here,
>   I say, shall die.
> Of all this world both far and near,
>   The lord am I.[1]

Herod's confidence that he and he alone defined truth was at least partly responsible for a number of judicial decisions that flew in the face of all "factual" evidence. The most chilling example of divine Herod's refusal to be constrained by any truths other than his own was the drumhead trial and execution of his second wife Mariamme and three of his own children.[2] The crime for which they fell was high treason. Granted, there was no clear-cut proof of their complicity. But all-knowing, truth-eating Herod declared them guilty, and so they were. His will determined truth in this as in all other cases. It's not that Herod cynically pretended that what he knew to be false was true. No, whatever he declared true *became* true simply by virtue of his lordly fiat. Truth was no longer objective or transcendent; devoured by the great God Herod, it became Herodian.

This propensity to truth-eating is apparent in today's God-luster. He blusters and struts less than Herod, of course; flamboyant displays of truth-eating are out of fashion. Instead, the contemporary Godluster generally adopts one of two strategies. Either he finesses his usurpation of Truth with philosophical appeals to subjectivism, assuring himself that truth doesn't exist independently of the human mind, and that what passes for truth in fact is only interpretation, an imaginative attempt on the part of the private intellect and will to bestow order and coherence on an otherwise meaningless universe. Or he simply digs in his heels, defiantly refusing to allow anyone to "tell him what to think," mulishly insisting that his opinions and interpretations are impregnable. His "truths" cannot be challenged by competing ones, nor is he obliged to bind himself to the "truths" of past generations. If *he* posits something as true, then it's true *for him*, and that's good enough.

However it's fleshed out, the contemporary truth-eater's seizure of truth as the prerogative of the self is precisely the move Herod made. The consequences are also identical: In relocating the source of truth from God to humans, God becomes an absent referent and humans become God—or so Godlusters hope. But as we saw in chapter 1, the demonic corruption of God-desire into Godlust is destructive. The Godluster cannot devour God, and his frenzied gorging so exiles him from God's saving presence that the ontological anxiety that originally drove him to rebel only sharpens. He aims for the empyrean heights, but is swallowed by the abyss.

In this chapter we'll explore more fully how truth-devouring destroys rather than divinizes us. But first let's get a better idea of what it means to devour truth by turning to a couple of its foremost champions. The first is the nineteenth-century iconoclast Friedrich Nietzsche. The second is the contemporary thinker Richard Rorty. Both men offer philosophical legitimations of truth-eating that, directly or indirectly, have exerted colossal influence on those today who lust for self-divinization. Together, they've made Original Sin respectable.

Come l'uom s'eterna

It was Friedrich Nietzsche, that eloquent and tormented singer of God's death, who in his doctrine of "perspectivism" gave the modern age its first systematic legitimation of the drive to eat and thus become Truth.[3] Perspectivism denies any objective grounding to truth or meaning. All that exists are personal interpretations or "perspectives." So-called truth is nothing more than an invention of our own making.

Just what Nietzsche meant by a "perspective" is unclear. Normally the word implies the reality of an independent state of affairs that individual inquirers, coming from various perspectives or points of view, labor to describe more or less accurately. But whatever else Nietzsche means by "perspective," it's not this. For him, there is no objective backdrop to our various interpretations; "no," he insists, "facts are precisely what there is *not*." There are only the interpretations or inventions themselves, and the perspective or point of view from which the subject creates them is her own private will and imagination. "Truth is therefore not something *there* that might be found or discovered—but something that must be created."[4]

Most people before and after Nietzsche concede that a good deal of what we know and say can only be expressed in symbolic or interpretive language, particularly when it comes to elusive religious, metaphysical, or ethical intuitions. But they balk at the conclusion that these interpretations are totally contrived. Instead, they argue, religious or ethical language gestures at, even if it cannot clearly mirror, objective truth. Saint Paul maintained (1 Cor 13:12) that we *do* see, even if only through a glass darkly. In a similar vein, Peter Berger reminds us that reality itself isn't relativized simply because our attempts to know and utter it are necessarily relative.[5] But Nietzsche has no patience with this position; not for him such timid half-measures. "Metaphysics, religion, moralities," he declares, "all of these are the offspring of…art[ifice], [of] falsehood."[6] They may possess a certain aesthetic elegance or psychological appeal, but in no way point to a truth beyond themselves. How could they? There's nothing there to point to.

Nietzsche's perspectivism doesn't stop here. Much more radically, he also dismisses the possibility of an objective grounding for science and logic. These too are merely symbolic or interpretive artifices contrived by humans. Physics is "only an interpretation of the world and an arrangement of it (to suit ourselves, if I may say so!)—and not an explanation of it," and if the world appears logical it's only "because *we* first *logicized* it."[7] So it's not just elusive religious and metaphysical beliefs that are inventions; "universal" assumptions about the physical realm, as well as the "laws" of logic and mathematics, likewise lack objective truth. No statement of any kind uttered by humans can be said to refer to an actual state of affairs. The only reality we dwell in and know is the one we spin for ourselves. "The world that we have not reduced to terms of our own being, our own logic, our psychological prejudices and presuppositions, does not exist as a world at all."[8] Instead, reality is merely fantasy, a rich tapestry of perspectival colors—and we are the colorists.

If objective truth is illusory, a mere projection of the imaginative will, then what we call "truth" is nothing more than a "mobile army of metaphors, metonymies, anthropomorphisms."[9] And what of meaning? It likewise is an invention, a contrived system of coherence constructed by human will rather than discovery. The first chapter of Genesis tells us that in the beginning God willed truth and meaning as extensions of his divine essence: *Let there be light, let there be firmament and waters, let there be heaven and earth, let there be creatures and humans!* The gospel according to Nietzsche recounts a similar story of creation. The only difference is that it's now *human* will that births truth and meaning and thereby breathes the world into being. And this, of course, means that humans have become God.

Timid souls may cower at Nietzsche's revelation that they and they alone are responsible for the creation of truth. For them, the disappearance of objective ground on which to stand proves too unsettling. But for the Herods of the world, the collapse of truth into perspectival interpretation is an occasion for great rejoicing. If God/Truth is dead, if there is no objective (much less transcendent) standard of truth to which our intellects and wills must bend, then we're free to define truth and meaning however we wish. We have finally reached our majority and are no longer bound by the will of the God-Parent. Nietzsche can barely contain his jubilation over the passing of authority from the old God to the new:

> Indeed, we philosophers and "free spirits" feel, when we hear the news that "the old god is dead," as if a new dawn shone on us; our heart overflows with gratitude, amazement, premonition, expectations. At long last the horizon appears free to us again.[10]

In a perspectival world devoid of independent truth and meaning, the new dawn Nietzsche proclaims doesn't shine *on* so much as it radiates *from* the almighty self, the new sun of the perspectival solar system we call "reality." It is this creative self, this imperious ego, that wills into being what is true and meaningful or determines what is false and meaningless. The self is the new alpha and omega.

And what's the motive for the self's invention of truth and meaning? Although Nietzsche plays around with several explanations, the one he returns to time and again is lust, or what he only a bit less candidly calls the "will to power." We create truth and meaning to suit ourselves, and what best suits us is anything that asserts and extends the divine power we covet and seek to gain in our God- and truth-eating. Nietzsche makes no bones about what's going on here. "It is *our* needs that interpret the world," he asserts, "*our* drives and their For and Against. Every drive is a kind of lust to rule," an insatiable obsession to streamroll all competing truths into submission. But far from condemning the obsession as an unwarranted usurpation of divine prerogative, Nietzsche celebrates it as the first shot in the human struggle to shuck off mortality and divinize the self. In his eyes, truth-eating is not a fall from grace. Cynically ripping a line out of Dante, Nietzsche claims that on the contrary it is *"Come l'uom s'eterna"*: "how man makes himself eternal."[11]

De-divinizing the World

Nietzsche the God-slayer is ruthlessly frank in his celebration of truth-eating. It's not enough, he insisted, merely to kill God. Humans must also muster the courage to go the full distance. They must belly up to the table and swallow the slain deity in order to take for themselves his qualities. Otherwise, the unforgiveable guilt of deicide cannot be borne. But Nietzsche was astute enough to realize that Godlusters less intrepid than he might choke on the sheer audacity of such advice. Two millennia of Christian "blessed are the meek" brain-washing has conditioned many would-be Godlusters to recoil on a conscious level to the lust that subconsciously quickens their pulse. Since truth-eaters have often found it so difficult to stomach his fiercely belligerent tone, Nietzsche predicted they would devise ways to sugarcoat it in less bitter cadences.

The American philosopher Richard Rorty's defense of truth-eating is a case in point. Rorty is easily one of the half dozen or so most influential thinkers of our day. He has both voiced and helped legitimize the modern Godluster's attempt to embrace Nietzsche's perspectival ingestion of Truth without duplicating the harshness of its rhetoric.

Rorty's starting point is the same as Nietzsche's: truth is not "out there" waiting to be discovered. This isn't because Rorty denies, as Nietzsche apparently does, that reality exists independently of us. He's perfectly content to agree with the commonsense intuition that somehow, in some way, "the world is out there, that it is not our creation [and] that most things in space and time are the effects of causes which do not include human mental states."[12] But Rorty insists that we must draw a distinction between claiming that the *world* is "out there" and that *truth* is "out there." The traditional assumption is that there's an inseparable connection between the two: We know truth because we discover it in the world. Rorty wants to sever this connection.

His reasoning is based on the conviction that there's no deep significance to words like *truth* or *meaning*, even though we pretend there is by tingeing them with a mystical aura. Truth and meaning are nothing more than properties of language. Sentences may be true or meaningful, but the world never is. Whatever else the "out-there" world may be, it simply isn't the sort of thing that possesses such properties:

> Truth cannot be out there—cannot exist independently of the human mind—because sentences cannot so exist, or be out there. The world is out there, but descriptions of the world are not. Only descriptions of the world can be true or false. The world on its own—unaided by describing activities of human beings—cannot.[13]

Thus the world is not the final arbiter between true and false statements, which is just to say that there is no objective criterion of truth to be discovered "out there." Yet we obviously designate some sentences as true or meaningful and others as false or meaningless. So what's the standard for this determination? Rorty thinks it's language itself. Every society generates a number of discourse contexts that contrive arbitrary rules for determining when the sentences used in them are properly designated as "true" or "false" and "meaningful" or "meaningless." These rules have no more to do with anything "out there" than, for example, the artificial rules of a game such as chess. A chess piece is defined in terms of the moves it can and cannot make. It's "true," for example, that a queen can move in any direction and that pawns cannot. But these "truths" that enable us to play chess clearly aren't reflections of any objective state of affairs. They're based simply on arbitrary game rules that chess players themselves invent and agree upon, and that in principle they're perfectly free to ignore or change if they desire. Chess "truths" have no more solid foundation, no deeper roots, than this.

Analogously, *any* discourse context is governed by equally arbitrary game rules that dictate truth and meaning for it. In the language game of logic, for example, the law of identity stipulates that it's "true" to affirm that something is identical to itself and "false" to deny it. In a similar vein, one of the stipulations of the language game of social liberalism decrees that it's meaningful to behave in such a way as to maximize tolerance for the opinions of others. But the law of identity is "true" and tolerance "meaningful" in these cases not because they somehow reflect objective truth, but because they are posited as true and meaningful by the players of the logic and liberalism games. Truth and meaning everywhere are simply properties of the contrived rules that dictate how language ought to be used in various contexts. They are completely relative to the cultural language game one happens to be playing.

It follows from the claim that truth and meaning are merely properties of language that humans are the final arbiters of what is true and what is meaningful. As Rorty points out, "To say that truth is not out there is simply to say that where there are no sentences there is no truth, that sentences are elements of human languages, and that human languages are human creations."[14] Since we invent language, and since truth and meaning ride on language, we also invent truth and meaning: Such is the conclusion to which Rorty's analysis leads. This echoes Nietzsche's insistence that just as language is fluid and ever changing, so are truth and meaning. And like Nietzsche, Rorty recommends that we get used to this because it's all we have. Truth is not a "deep matter," and pretending otherwise is as "unprofitable" as pretending that words such as "human nature" or "God" gesture at transcendent Truth or fixed meaning. They do not, and when we accept this we throw over absolutely nothing of substance. On the contrary, says Rorty, we jettison a mythical "world well lost."[15]

Nietzsche saw his perspectivism as emancipatory because he believed it empowered humans to create truth and meaning without the tedious interference of a God. Rorty takes his reduction of truth and meaning to linguistic properties as equally liberating. The notion that truth exists independently of the human mind or will, he claims, "is a remnant of the idea that the world is a divine creation, the work of someone who had something in mind, who Himself spoke some language in which He described His own project." Drop this notion, Rorty promises, and we rid ourselves of the stifling burden of truth and meaning imposed on us from the outside. When we take this step, we "de-divinize the world."[16] And in de-divinizing the world, in assuming for ourselves the prerogative of inventing truth and meaning—which of course is just Rorty-ese for absent-referencing God—we eat Truth and thereby divinize ourselves.

In their separate but related ways, Nietzsche and Rorty offer contemporary Godlusters thoroughgoing philosophical justifications of truth-eating. Their two models aren't precisely identical. Nietzsche's focus is on the way *individuals* eat truth and thereby become its source, while Rorty emphasizes the way humans dwelling together in various *discourse contexts* eat and thereby define truth. But both formulations are ultimately driven by the same demonic lust to wrest Truth from God and subject it to human sovereignty. For Nietzsche as well as Rorty, the goal is to slay the rival Other and de-divinize creation so that humans may devour the Tree of Knowledge without fear of interference or rebuke.

The Beholding Eye

John Berendt's best-selling *Midnight in the Garden of Good and Evil* is a real-life whodunit about a 1981 slaying that rocked the city of Savannah, Georgia. Jim Williams, an antiques dealer notorious for both his luxurious lifestyle and his extravagant high-society Christmas parties, shot and killed young Danny Hansford, an employee who also happened to be his lover. Williams claimed it was self-defense, but the local authorities thought otherwise and charged him with murder. The case stayed in the courts for almost a decade, passing through conviction, appeal, mistrial, and eventual acquittal, and the stories surrounding the killing became legion and legendary. When the trials finally ended, everyone had so dug in his or her heels that nobody much cared any longer about the "facts" of Danny

Hansford's death. The DA doggedly continued to claim that Williams was guilty of murder; Williams's official response was that he had fired only after Danny drunkenly assaulted him; off the record, Williams told one or two people a darker, more incriminating account of what happened; and in the meantime, everyone else in Savannah settled on his or her own pet theory about the shooting.

Jim Williams died in 1990, and so questions about Danny Hansford's slaying will forever remain unanswered. *Midnight in the Garden of Good and Evil* takes this unresolved and now unresolvable mystery as the occasion to make a larger point: that the world contains stories, opinions, interpretations, and perceptions, but not objective truth. Everybody's got his or her own personal spin on truth, and one's just as good as another. (The additional implication is that this is actually a lucky break, because stories are so much more entertaining than mere "facts" anyway.) A final scene in the film version of the book states this subjectivism in a clear although somewhat heavy-handed fashion. Jim Williams is asked shortly before his death if he ever plans to tell the "truth" about what *really* happened on the night Danny was killed. "Truth, like art," Williams smilingly replies, "is in the eye of the beholder. You believe what you want to believe."

Jim Williams probably never read Nietzsche or Rorty, yet his reduction of truth to subjective preference reflects the tendency of philosophy to trickle down into popular culture and conveniently legitimize what we already wish to maintain. When Williams asserts that truth is in the beholding eye, his utterance is a layperson's version of the truth-eating abstractly defended by the likes of Nietzsche and Rorty. What passes for truth is nothing more than interpretive spin, and the spin in turn is generated by what the interpreting subject deems in his or her best interest to believe. The DA's truth is that Hansford's killing was premeditated murder, Williams's truth (or at least one of them) is that it was self-defense, and the man and woman in the street's truth is whichever story best tickles his or her fancy. In a universe stripped of objective truth, what standards are left except personal preference or the consensus of whichever discourse context we happen to find ourselves in?

Each age comes up with its own justifications for truth-eating. For contemporary Godlusters, the subjectivism defended by thinkers such as Nietzsche and Rorty is the frame of reference consciously or unconsciously appealed to. Herod's shameless touting of his own divinity is passé. But necessity is ever the mother of invention, and today's Godluster finds a more sympatico vehicle in the trickle-down notion that truth and meaning are in the eye of the beholder. Truth as perspective, subjective inclination, story, invention, social construct, linguistic property: This is the appropriate idiom of modern truth-eating.

Everyday patterns of speech suggest just how pervasive the trickle-down is. We say things like "It's all just a matter of opinion!" or "You're just playing word games!" when cornered in debate. If confounded by data, we sullenly mutter, "You can do anything you want with numbers and statistics!" We protect our assumed roles as truth-inventors with pseudolibertarian phrases such as "Don't impose your truth on me!" and "I have a right to my own opinion!" We glibly talk about spin doctors, angles of vision, and paradigms, and we toss around the modifier *relative* (as in "all truth is relative") at the slightest provocation. Along with jaded Qoheleth, who concluded that there's no real difference between folly and wisdom (Eccl 2:14–15), we modern Godlusters are too savvy to be hedged in by "objective" truth. We've outgrown the naive conviction that truth and meaning exist independently of subjective will or cultural language games. There are only stories. Admittedly, some may be more entertaining than others; but for all that, they are still, one and all, just stories. And we are the storytellers.

It can hardly be denied that the historical period in which we live encourages the attitude that truth is in the eye of the beholder. The information revolution that began with radio and television and has now graduated to computer technology bombards us with exponentially accelerating waves of competing ideas, theories, worldviews, and values. As Alvin Toffler pointed out almost a generation ago, the incessant demand for judgments that this dizzying onrush of divergent information makes on our intellects is more than most of us can bear. It so threatens to short-circuit us that we defensively shut down and tune out.[17] One of the most convenient ways to do this is to adopt the truth-eating attitude expressed by Jim Williams: "Truth, like art, is in the eye of the beholder." If we assume that truth is subjective, then we need not be smothered under the avalanche of rival truth-claims vying for our allegiance. We reassert our autonomy and control by creating our own "truths" and ignoring all the others.

But the unsettling psychological effects of the contemporary information explosion are occasions rather than causes of the urge to eat truth. While it's undeniable that the current information whirlwind exacerbates our anxious sense of inadequacy, it's also the case that its disorienting effects feed into an underlying distress more ontological than psychological: the worm of Godlust. The numbed impression that reality is a bewildering hodgepodge of subjective and contextual interpretations may be encouraged by the computer age, but our opportunistic Godlust takes this as an entrée to declare the self sovereign when it comes to truth.

The Most to Be Pitied

When we eat truth we take for ourselves the divine prerogative of Truth-decreeing and transform the self's beholding eye
into the exclusive source of truth and meaning. The hope is
that this usurpation will cure the ontological anxiety bred by
our deiformic sense of separateness; this is the ultimate victory coveted by the Godlusting heart. But as we saw in chapter 1, Godlust's drive toward self-divinization is actually a
demonic attempt to absolutize the finite and so is both futile
and destructive. To paraphrase Saint Paul (1 Cor 15:19), if the
self is the fount of truth, then we are the most to be pitied.
When we look to it for a way out of ontological anxiety, we
look in vain. The self as source of truth is a sorry substitute for
the Truth of God. It simply isn't up to the job.

Simone Weil reminds us of the self's inability to proxy for
God by focusing on what she calls its "mediocrity."

> Religion teaches that God created finite beings of differ-
> ent degrees of mediocrity. We human beings are aware
> that we are at the extreme limit, the limit beyond which
> it is no longer possible to conceive or to love God. Below
> us there are only the animals. We are as mediocre and as
> far from God as it is possible for creatures endowed with
> reason to be.[18]

Weil measures a being's worth by its ontological proximity
to the Creator and rather dismally concludes that humans, sit-
uated as we are at the extreme edge of God-awareness, push
the envelope. What she refers to as mediocrity obviously is
another way of stating our deiformic separateness from God.
Her use of the word *mediocre* also grippingly underscores the
self's abysmal inadequacy for grounding Truth.

Whatever else can be said about the self, unhappy experience teaches us that it is whimsical, conflicted, seducible, and fallible. It weathercocks from one passion to another, from one stimulus to the next, with hardly a pause in between. Often the self is torn in a number of different directions, frenetically trying to hold onto two or more incompatible beliefs. All this makes the self particularly prone to error and misjudgment. What's more, the self stubbornly resists learning from past mistakes. It has an enormous capacity for self-deception, particularly when it comes to the pursuit of harmful desires. The self, in short, is a fumbler, an Inspector Clouseau-like entity that manages to get by, but just barely. It is, as Weil says, mediocre.

When the truth-eating Godluster attempts to absolutize this mediocre self as the ultimate Ground of truth, the kind of "truth" he's left with sadly reflects its source. The "truth" it generates is fragmented, contingent, foundationless, and limited. Nietzsche may gleefully proclaim that perspectives are perfectly satisfactory substitutes for objective truth and meaning. But in fact they are horrifyingly fragile because utterly dependent upon a self that flits from one interpretation to the next. Rorty may solemnly declare that the "out-there" world is one well lost because only language creates truth and meaning. But since language is a human creation, it necessarily carries with it the creating self's unreliable mediocrity, once more underscoring the shakiness of the divinized self's "truth." Jim Williams may glibly claim that truth is in the eye of the beholder. But if the eye is flawed, what then of truth? "If your eye is not sound, your whole body will be full of darkness" (Mt 6:23).

A cynic might shrug her shoulders and put up with the slippery truth generated by the mediocre self. If that's all there is, that's all there is, and one should learn to live with it. But the Godluster isn't a cynic. He's consumed with a ravenous appetite for the Absolute, and nothing less substantial will satisfy him. Distanced from the divine Source of Truth first by his deiformic separateness and then by his own misguided rapacity, frustration torments him until out of sheer desperation he tries to eat and thereby absorb what he so craves: Absolute Truth. But he can neither eat it nor absorb it; the demonic attempt to absolutize the finite cannot succeed. So the Godluster's frenzy to make his mediocre self the sole standard of Truth leaves him with a nightmarish parody more alienating than the inadequacy he seeks to escape.

All sin is destructive, and the Original Sin of Godlust is most destructive of all. The truth-eating by which Godlust aims to achieve self-divinization only drives the hurting, yearning soul deeper into the forlorn abyss. Nietzsche and Rorty are wrong. God's death knell doesn't sound emancipation for humans. It tolls *our* destruction, because it necessarily drives us back upon our selves. And as Weil tells us, those selves are mediocre substitutes for the Absolute Being we crave.

But the doomed obsession to eat truth isn't the last word. Godlust after all is the shadow side of God-desire. We can wallow in the despair of separateness and start down the demonic way of self-divinization, or we can "wake from sleep" (Rom 13:11) and embrace our connectedness, progressively growing into the deification God intends for us. If we choose the second path, the Truth we encounter is quite different from the Godluster's. It is not in the eye of the beholder; it cannot be willed into existence. It is not just a perspective or an interpretation. It's not a property of sentences within discourse contexts. Nor is it merely a common sense correspondence between intellect and fact. Instead, the Truth we encounter is God's unconcealment. It is *aletheia.*

Aletheia

The word typically used by the ancient Greeks when they talked about truth was *aletheia.* New Testament authors, especially John, also used it when speaking of Jesus or recording his words: "I am the way, and the truth [*aletheia*], and the life...."; "Sanctify them in the truth [*aletheia*]...."; "...you will know the truth [*aletheian*], and the truth [*aletheia*] will make you free" (Jn 14: 6; 17:17; 8:32).

The word *aletheia,* like its English counterpart, has several meanings. Sometimes it suggests "certainty" or "trustworthiness." Paul is especially fond of this connotation. In his letter to the Galatians (2:5), for instance, he says that his mission is to work so that "the **trustworthiness** [*aletheia*]of the gospel might be preserved." Later in the same epistle (2:14) he speaks of the "**certainty** of the gospel" (*aletheian tou euaggeliou*). In his letter to Ephesus (4:21) he urges the faithful to put their ultimate trust in Jesus because Jesus alone is ultimately **trustworthy** (*aletheia en to Iesou*).

Elsewhere the New Testament uses *aletheia* to suggest "honesty" or the "opposite of duplicity." The author of 1 Timothy (2:7) assures his or her audience that "I am telling the **honest** truth [*aletheian*], I am not lying." Paul likewise asks the church at Corinth (1 Cor 7:14) to believe that the good news he brings them is "the **honest** truth" (*aletheia*). John begins his second and third epistles by assuring his readers that he **honestly** loves them (*agapo en aletheia*).

On other occasions, the New Testament uses *aletheia* for the prosaic purpose of talking about the "facts" or "actual states of affairs." Perhaps the most famous passage that employs *aletheia* in this sense is recorded in John 18:38. There, Pilate asks Jesus if he's really the king of the Jews. Jesus' answer plays on *aletheia's* ambiguity: "Everyone who is of the truth hears my voice." Legalistic Pilate obtusely misunderstands Jesus' words, supposing that he means nothing more than "Whoever knows the facts of the case knows what I'm all about," and accordingly replies, "But what *are* the **facts?**" (*ti estin aletheia?*).

So far, the different meanings of *aletheia* found in the New Testament are pretty run-of-the-mill and correspond to the ordinary ways in which the English "truth" is used. But there is still another meaning of *aletheia*, one expressed in verses such as 1 John 2:8, where we read "I am writing you a new commandment, which is **real** [*alethes*] in Jesus and **real** [*alethes*] in you, because the darkness is passing away and the **real** [*alethinon*] light is shining," or in 1 John 5:7, where the author says that "the Spirit is **Reality**" (*aletheia*). These and other passages (e.g., Acts 12:9; Jn 14:6, 14:17, 16:13; 1 Jn 4:6) point to a deeper meaning of truth. They suggest that truth is a revelation which, like a shining beacon, illuminates the Real, that which truly *is* rather than that which merely *seems* to be. (Scripture translations in this paragraph are the author's.)

Sometimes, then, *aletheia* refers to commonplace experiences of trustworthiness or honesty or facticity. But at its most profound level, it is the sudden *unconcealment* of absolute Reality, of pure Being. And for the New Testament, the absolute Reality that is unconcealed by *aletheia* is none other than God. Truth is God's act of unveiling. When we experience this unveiling, this unconcealing, we encounter Truth.

If we unpack this notion of *aletheia* as unconcealment of ultimate Reality, we discover that it has three aspects or moments. A*letheia* refers to the *gracious event* of unconcealment, to the *bringing-forth* of that which was concealed, and to our *response* to that which has been brought forth.

Aletheia as Gracious Event. Contrary to the claims of truth-eaters such as Nietzsche and Rorty, Truth is not something we cause to happen. Instead, it is an event—a "truthing," if you will—that happens to us, a fateful and decisive opportunity for insight (*kairos*) created by God in order to draw us farther along the path of the deification that is our destiny. This event is an intrusion into the ordinary, a revelatory moment in which the doors of spiritual perception are thrown open and the heavens unfold before us. A*letheia* in this sense is an outbreak of divine creativity, a nova-like rupture of the normal whose ensuing intensity and brilliance sweeps us away. God's self-disclosure in the Genesis account of creation and atop Mount Sinai; God's self-unveiling to the Hebrew prophets; God's unconcealing to Peter, John, and James on Mount Tabor, and to Paul on the Damascus Road: Each of these are examples of divine Being in the act of truthing. The pinnacle of such alethic happenings is, of course, the incarnation, the Christ-event in which God's creative presence unconceals to transfigure the ordinary once and forever.

What all these alethic unveilings have in common is that they are initiated by divine grace. The God-event of *aletheia* is a freely bestowed gift to humans that bridges our deiformic separateness and underscores our connectedness. Unable to reach up to God, God extends the divine Self to us, favoring us with an inrush of Truth, which, unaided, we can never attain through our own efforts. Far from being a Moloch-like deity who takes without giving, God joyfully exposes his Truth to us in an act of supreme Love. As we'll discover in chapter 4, such an alethic self-giving lies at the heart of divine Goodness.

Aletheia as Bringing-Forth. When the decisive event of truthing occurs, what was previously hidden or concealed or veiled from the human spirit is brought forth. God reveals God's presence in the alethic moment, which is just to say that Reality as it really is unveils before us. From the truthing of *aletheia* as gracious event is brought forth Truth, that which is profoundly and ultimately Real. Perhaps the most dramatic scriptural account of this bringing-forth of the Truth is the story of Moses' encounter with the burning bush on Mount Horeb's slope (Ex 3:14). God unconceals God in that moment of truthing as the plenitudinous "I AM"—Being Itself, absolute Reality. (Recall the point made in chapter 1 that Yahweh seems to be derived from the Hebrew *hawah*, "to be.") God is that which IS in the deepest sense of the word, and when we encounter this IS, we have encountered Truth.

In the Christian dispensation, if the Incarnation is the truthing-event, Jesus is the Truth thereby unconcealed or brought forth. Jesus is not merely the reflection or image of divine Being/Truth. Jesus *is* divine Being/Truth. In Jesus God IS, and in encountering Jesus we encounter the I AM. "Truly, truly, I say to you, before Abraham was, I am" (Jn 8:58). The apostle John's greatest insight was his recognition of this divine unconcealment in Jesus the Christ, the way, the *aletheia*, and the life.

It is a commonplace that truthing-events rarely bring forth divine Truth in the overwhelming manner of a Mount Horeb or Damascus Road experience. God/Truth, we tell ourselves, seldom unconceals in such a dramatic fashion. But this is a mistaken assumption. Whenever *aletheia* happens, it is the same cosmic revelation of Being that nearly consumed Moses or Paul. God is God, and any divine self-disclosure carries with it the full weight of Reality. If we fail to experience such decisive moments in our own lives, it's not because God's acts of unconcealing wax and wane in intensity, but rather because we refuse to open ourselves to them. Whether alethic disclosure comes in the form of fire and thunder on Sinai, or whether it comes as more "ordinary" signals of transcendence such as trustworthiness, honesty, and facticity that point beyond themselves to ultimate Truth, the revelation is the same. The rub is acquiring eyes with which to see and ears with which to hear.

Aletheia as Response. When we open ourselves to the unconcealment of supreme Truth we become possessed by it. Our entire being is suffused by its Presence and we live in *aletheia*, in the Truth (1 Jn 1:6). The encounter is not primarily intellectual. Our intellects, in fact, are quite inadequate to grasp what has happened to us. How could they, finite and limited as they are? Reason is capable of understanding truths, but not Truth itself. Intelligence can grasp what it means for individual objects to be, but is left stunned by the revelation of absolute Being. In God's bringing-forth of Truth, we encounter that which can be experienced but not understood.

In a recent book on Job, Richard Rohr suggests that "truth is more a person than an idea."[19] This is an insightful observation, because when we respond to *aletheia*, we do so in an existential rather than an intellectual way. As in our encounters with living persons, we live rather than merely think about the relationship. Our entire being instead of just our mind is changed. As Kierkegaard puts it, "Christianly understood, truth is obviously not to *know* the truth but to *be* the truth,"[20] and this is because Truth, like persons, is ultimately a Mystery that defies facile classification. Deep within the core of every unconcealment lies that which forever remains concealed. As Augustine noted, when Truth "is present" it shows itself as a "public" yet also "mysteriously secret" light.[21] We cannot find words or conceptual categories to express this supreme Reality. "To whom then will you liken god, or what likeness compare him with?" (Is 40:18). Truth's absolute plenitude defies the mind's usual strategies of classification and definition, and we know with rock-bottom certainty that we stand in the presence of something that we could not have originated and that we cannot command: "...you cannot say that immutable truth is yours, or mine, or anyone else's."[22] Instead, observes Karl Rahner, we are overtaken "by what no longer has a name [and] is not mastered but is itself the master. [*Aletheia*] is the speech of the [B]eing without a name, about which clear statements are not possible."[23] Consequently, when we *do* try to speak the alethic Mystery, we necessarily fall back onto metaphors and poetic similes that stumble woefully short of the mark. Contrary to Rorty, Truth is not a property of language, but rather that which transcends all attempts to utter it.

Speechless as our response to unconcealment must be, it nonetheless is replete with awareness and insight. We feel it even if we don't comprehend that we stand before the Holy and the Sacred, and the experience, as Rudolf Otto famously argued, engulfs us in awe and fascination.[24] We are electrified with the presence of the Completeness and Absoluteness for which our hearts yearn, and we fill with gratitude and adoration. We also fill with humility because we at last see that the mediocre self is hopelessly unable even to approximate such Reality/Truth. Finally, we sense that the Presence is saturated with graciousness and love, that it has unveiled itself to us out of unadulterated benevolence—that the unconcealment, in fact, is a self-giving. Our deiformic connectedness with God throbs to respond in kind and to reach out with our whole being in the *ek-stasis* of self-emptying love. We no longer want to seize and conquer. We are *in* the Truth and now wish only to give in return. "We love because God first loved us" (1 Jn 4:19), and that original divine love is part of the Mystery *aletheia* brings forth. (We'll return to this point in chapter 4.)

Indiferença

God is Truth, and when God unconceals, Truth is unconcealed. *Aletheia* is a divine boon graciously offered us to reawaken our sense of deiformic connectedness and draw us into the deification that is our destiny. Truth, like grace, abounds. As one of the worldly signals of transcendence, its vestiges are encountered everywhere: in moments of honesty, certainty, trustworthiness, facticity, and in "aha" experiences of intellectual insight that leave us breathless. God's/Truth's presence permeates the fabric of our experience, patiently coaxing us away from the here-and-now anxiety that breeds Godlust.

But God is not a drillmaster who insists on marching us willy-nilly where he desires we should go. It's quite true that we are innately drawn to God and God's ways. Our deiformic affinity, God's great gift to us, predisposes us to God-desire long before we are consciously aware of it. Each of us is called from the womb. But it's equally true that God will not force us to himself. Coerced liberation is just a disguised form of enslavement; mandated love is no love at all. Consequently, we must take some responsibility for our spiritual growth. We must sensitize ourselves to our essential connectedness with the Divine, honestly explore its depths, awaken to our inherent God-desire, gratefully assent to it, and actively cooperate with God's plan of deification. The soul's journey to God is a collaborative partnership: God lovingly initiates and encourages our pilgrimage; we choose the gift and struggle to be worthy of it. In one of his letters, Saint Ignatius of Loyola sketched the structure of this partnership. "It is a mistake," he wrote, "to rely upon oneself and to place one's hope in any resources or exertions for their own sakes. Conversely, it is not a sure way to rely on God our Lord alone, without allowing myself to be helped by what He has given me."[25]

But how do we do this? How do we make a choice *against* truth-eating and *for* cooperation with the divine invitation to embrace our innate connectedness with Truth/God? Ignatius gives us a clue at the beginning of his *Spiritual Exercises*, where he states that a first step in learning to "praise, reverence, and serve God" is to "make ourselves indifferent to all created things, insofar as it is left to the choice of our free will and is not forbidden." The cultivation of spiritual *indiferença* helps us "desire and choose only those things which will best help us attain the end for which we are created."[26] And that end, of course, is deification.

Ignatius' *indiferença* ought not to be equated with what we generally mean by "indifference," and I use the Spanish term to underscore the distinction. In ordinary language "indifference" suggests a listless attitude of apathy or careless indiscrimination. If I'm indifferent, I don't give enough of a damn to make an effort. I just can't be bothered. To be indifferent, then, is to succumb to the spiritual indolence that paralyzed world-weary Qoheleth.

But *indiferença* isn't a listless shrugging of the shoulders. There's nothing passive or apathetic about it. Instead, it is a spiritual state of extreme alertness, of responsiveness and readiness. It is a quivering of the nostrils and an arching of the ears. It is a perpetual expectancy of the advent of *aletheia*.

When Ignatius declares that the cultivation of *indiferençia* is necessary for attuning to the Divine's unconcealment, he has in mind a two-stage process. The first step is one of detachment, an "ultimate reserve and coolness towards all particular ways," as Karl Rahner puts it.[27] When we cultivate detachment, we strive to wean ourselves from the "particular" subjectivisms our wills-to-power posit as absolute truth, and which deflect our attention and desire away from *aletheia*. We refuse to take our mediocre selves as ultimate concerns, instead directing ultimate concern to where it properly belongs: God/Truth.

Rahner's description of *indiferençia's* initial stage as cool reserve shouldn't lead us to suppose that detachment is a dour repudiation of the joys of existence. A self-loathing and flesh-punishing asceticism is often as much a form of pride as Godlust, and just as predictably can blind us to the alethic presence of the Divine. Life is for living, and the adoption of a standoffish contempt for the pleasures of everyday existence frequently betokens an unseemly and somewhat voyeuristic timidity. Genuine detachment doesn't condemn worldly objects and objectives so much as it puts them in proper perspective by reminding us that any genuine attractiveness they possess is borrowed from God. This being the case, the person of detachment neither fixates on them as ultimate concerns nor despises them as somehow inherently evil. They come from God and point back to their Source, and detachment appreciates them for what they are.

When seen in this light, detachment becomes a vehicle of rejoicing and fulfillment rather than dreary, teeth-gritting suffering. A refusal to detach in fact *occasions* suffering, because it scatters our energy and distracts our attention from what's in our best interest. The self that has not put its own cravings in proper perspective is in grave danger of taking them as ultimate concerns. But this path leads to the oppressive sense of inadequacy that sparks Godlust in the first place because the mediocre self, although not an evil in itself, is unable to satisfy our profoundest longings.

Detachment clears the way for clarity, liberation, and empowerment, each of which is necessary for the soul's journey to God. It clarifies by enabling us to distance ourselves from the imperious ego and its wants long enough to realize that their inherent mediocrity is a pitifully unstable foundation for Truth. It liberates by helping us appreciate that the lust to absolutize the self through truth-eating in fact is a demonic form of bondage. Finally detachment empowers, because once we recognize the mediocre self's inadequacy and forsake the lust to become and define Truth, we acknowledge our weakness and thereby open ourselves up to the grace of *aletheia*. Jesus said "...my power is made perfect in weakness" (2 Cor 12:9). God's power, the power of absolute and eternal Truth, enters into us when we drop the self-imposed barriers of pride and self-sufficiency and confess our dependency. To do so is to face squarely our deiformic separateness and to experience the anguish of ontological anxiety. But detachment here as elsewhere helps us to put the forlornness of separateness in perspective. Instead of using it as an excuse for existential envy and Godlust, the person of detachment now embraces it as a sign of her need to seek completion in God. Feelings of inadequacy may endure, but they now become the routes on which the power of *aletheia* travels. Weakness therefore is a radical openness that pushes back the clutter of Original Sin so that there's room for the life-giving spirit of God.

Once we reach the point of genuine detachment we're ready to graduate to the second stage of Ignatius's *indiferença*: an attentive waiting for the presence of God wherever (and that is *every*where) God wishes to be found, an alert and receptive readiness for the truthing-event of *aletheia*. Liberated from the nagging Godlust that focuses only on separateness, progressively filled with a God-desire that celebrates connectedness, we harken with mounting excitement and joy to the Truth that saturates the universe. Like Plato's cave dweller who climbs steadily upwards from darkness to light, the attentive soul more and more takes notice of the worldly signals of transcendence that point to Truth. No longer compelled by Godlust to seize and consume them, the soul on its way back to God gratefully recognizes them as landmarks along the way that point her in the right direction. The world becomes radiant, a wondrous and exhilarating thing suffused with the splendor of Truth and the joy of God. Life becomes the adventure it was intended to be, and we "rejoice in the Lord," as Saint Paul says (Phil 3:1).

There is a progression to deification, just as there is a progression to all growth. The more we wean ourselves from truth-eating and joyfully attend to God's truthing, the more we advance from glimpses of unconcealment in discrete signals of transcendence to the possibility of eventually standing in the full presence of what Rahner earlier described as "the [B]eing without a name, about which clear statements are not possible." As we've seen, this progression doesn't mean that there's a sliding scale of unconcealments ranging from partial to full intensity. When Truth unveils, it unveils.

Instead, the progression results from our steadily growing openness to *aletheia*.

Saint Augustine (for one) grew into such radical openness, but only after laboring mightily in what he called the "school of the heart." He tells us in his *Confessions* that his early youth was given over to Godlust and particularly to its mania to eat truth. His training in rhetoric and his immersion in the squabbles among various schools of philosophy had convinced him that truth was an illusion and that what passed for truth was merely the sophistical ability to persuade. But through what Ignatius would later call *indiferença*, Augustine gradually allowed the call of his deiformic connectedness to open his eyes to the traces of Truth unconcealed in the world about him. He graduated at last from these dim glimpses to an unimpeded vision of divine Truth/Reality. In attempting to say something about it he gives this description of the fruits of *indiferença's* alert readiness:

> If to anyone the tumult of the flesh has fallen silent, if the images of earth, water, and air are quiescent, if the heavens themselves are shut out and the very soul itself is making no sound and is surpassing itself by no longer thinking about itself, if all dreams and visions in the imagination are excluded, if all language and every sign and everything transitory is silent...then God alone would speak not through [created things] but through himself. We would hear his word, not through the tongue of the flesh, nor through the voice of an angel, nor through the sound of thunder, nor through the obscurity of a symbolic utterance. Him who in these things we love we would hear in person without their mediation.[28]

Reality as it is in itself, unfiltered through the prisms of our egoistic lust; Truth as it freely unconceals itself, rather than truth as an imperialistic extension of our will to power; the Absolute in all its unsayable, mysterious glory, rather than the tawdry self-divinizing pretensions of the Godluster: This is *aletheia*. This is what we yearn for. This is our destiny.

Living the Unconcealment

Demonic urges are unimaginative. The worm in the heart lacks either talent or power to create *de novo*. Instead, its specialty is corruption of the spiritual muscle in which it squirms. It mutates the raw material of God-desire into Godlust, perverts our natural longing for Truth into rapacious truth-eating, and twists our inherent awareness of dependency on God into bitter existential envy. Demonic distortion, consequently, is a caricature of the connectedness to God each of us carries within our hearts, and traces of that affinity can be discerned even in its worst perversions.

King Herod's arrogant attempt to define truth, Nietzsche's and Rorty's more subtle philosophical truth-eating, Jim Williams's beholding eye: Each of these are perversions that nonetheless gesture at a great insight. Herod and his fellow-travelers throughout the centuries futilely strive to eat and hence be Truth; this is one of the tactics of their campaign to become God. But this urge is the demonic nether side of a legitimate desire and a genuine possibility. We cannot absolutize the finite and make ourselves Truth, nor should we wish to do so. But we can and should hunger to become truths, and in fact such is the destiny of deiform creatures. This is just another way of saying that when we experience *aletheia* we are so possessed and transfigured by it that we live it, that it is existential in its effects rather than merely intellectual.

As I pointed out in chapter 1, our proper end is a steady growth into Godlikeness. This means that, with God's help, we seek to comport ourselves in the world in a Godly manner by imitating, to the best of our ability, divine Being. The God-luster fundamentally misunderstands what it is to be God and so attempts to become a God-who-devours, who takes without giving, and commands but disdains to serve. But this is not the God revealed in scripture or the God we are called to imitate. The God of Abraham, Sarah, and Rachel, the God incarnated in Jesus the Christ, is a God of self-giving and love, a God of such patience and concern, compassion and benevolence, that he willingly sacrifices himself for the sake of his wayward children. This God has emptied himself throughout the world—his unconcealment is everywhere, if we have eyes to see it—and this unconcealment serves as a Light in and to the world, a Light that shines in the darkness and is not conquered by the darkness. God's gift of himself in unconcealment is the "true Light [*to phos to alethinon*] that enlightens every person" (Jn 1:9).

Persons who experience the light of God's Truth are not only *illuminated* in the sense that they know *aletheia*. They also become *luminous* in that their very existence is radiated, shot through and through, by the Truth unconcealed to and for them. The alethic revelation of absolute Being so speaks to our heart's inner core that it transfigures our whole being. Just as God's Truth is the Light unto the world, so we, who now participate in its luminosity, become points of light. From being perceivers of God's signals of transcendence, we become signals of transcendence ourselves: We become truths that point beyond ourselves to the supreme Truth. We are remade by our experience of unconcealment into unconcealing-events for others. John says that "the Word became flesh and dwelt among us, full of grace and *aletheias*" (Jn 1:14). The Word continues to dwell in our midst whenever we live in *aletheia* and unconceal for others what has been unconcealed for us.

This is a heavy responsibility, for it demands of us that we give ourselves to God and to others in imitation of God's loving self-giving. As lights, we are called to burn ourselves out in the service of Light. As truths, we are called to strenuous acts of truthing in which we allow divine Truth to use us as the conduits through which it unconceals. When *aletheia* happens to us, it takes us and makes us its own. As Saint Maximos said, a divine interpenetration occurs: God/Truth enters us in order that we might become God-/Truth-like.

Yet the responsibility of living the Truth to which Christians are called is also a great blessing, for it is the only way to satisfy the God-desire with which we are born. The Godluster thinks his hunger can be assuaged if he devours God. He fears that the subordination of his craving will to the Truth will enslave him. But he predictably has things backwards. God-desire is satisfied only when we allow ourselves to be taken by God. As Augustine points out, freedom actually consists in "submission to the Truth," because the Truth is God and "it is our God Himself who frees us from death, that is, from the state of sin."[29] Herod the God-eater, Herod the Truth-eater, would find this patent nonsense. But anyone who has experienced the alethic moment of unconcealment and thereby lives in the Truth knows better.

Chapter Three

Godlust and Beauty

Lord am I of sea and sand;
All earthly things bow to my hand.

Herod

One thing have I asked of the Lord,
that I will seek after: …to behold
the beauty of the Lord.

Psalm 27

Conqueror of Nature

King Herod was a master builder. History best remembers his construction of the Second Temple, that splendid edifice wantonly destroyed by Titus when he sacked Jerusalem in 70 C.E. But for all its magnificence, the Temple was by no means Herod's greatest engineering and architectural accomplishment. Miles south of Jerusalem, where the Judean Desert drops into the Dead Sea, Herod leveled a mountaintop and constructed the palace-fortress of Masada. Further north, not far from Bethlehem, he reversed procedure to raise an artificial cone-shaped mountain that he promptly topped off with another palace-fortress he called Herodium. And in the north of his kingdom, about fifteen miles south of modern-day Haifa, Herod subdued the ocean just as he'd conquered the land by building the Mediterranean city of Caesarea Maritima.

Leveling or raising mountains is no small feat, but both dwarf in comparison to what Herod did at Caesarea. A small harbor town had been on the site for a few hundred years. By the first century it had pretty much decayed, leaving the entire northern coastline without a haven for trading vessels. Herod decided to remedy this by resurrecting the town. When he took on the project, however, he discovered that the Mediterranean Sea had other ideas. As Josephus described the situation, "even a moderate breeze dashes the waves against the rocks with such force that the backflow churns up the sea far off the coast." But what were wind and waves to mighty Herod? In less than ten years he tamed the stormy waters by sinking tons of stone into them in order to create a colossal breakwater and harbor. When finished, it provided even deeper anchorage than the Piraeus, Athen's famous harbor. "Thus," announced Josephus, "Herod conquered nature herself."[1]

How typical of Herod, this assertion of sovereignty over sea and sand. He saw the natural world as just another realm to be seized, subdued, and stamped with his royal seal. The weapons he used were intellectual—geometry, mechanical engineering, mathematics—supplemented by the brute strength of thousands of forced laborers. And these weapons got the job done. They leveled or raised mountains, held back the seas, carved stone, defied gravity. They reduced the physical realm to ready-to-hand victuals for Herod to swallow and make his own. With them, Herod conquered and appropriated nature, thereby establishing suzerainty over it. The massive fortresses with which he dotted the landscape were not only safeguards against human unruliness; they were also symbols of his war against physical creation.

Herod's lust to dominate and re-create nature isn't just royal hubris. More significantly, it's symptomatic of a hunger every bit as demonic as truth-eating. When he eats truth, the Godluster refuses to open himself to those truth-conveying signals of transcendence that gesture at the Truth of divine Being. Instead of allowing them to draw him out of himself toward God, he sees them as challenges to his self-divinization and sets up his own will in opposition to them. In a similar fashion, the Godluster refuses to acknowledge the signals of transcendence that abound in the natural realm because they too threaten his assumed Godhood. So, like Herod, he goes on the offensive by proclaiming himself lord of sea and sand.

The signal of transcendence on which Godlust declares war when it seeks to conquer nature is beauty. The Hebrew and Christian traditions both teach that just as God is Supreme Truth, so God is also Absolute Beauty. Divine Truth is reflected, even if only dimly, in human experiences of truth such as honesty, facticity, and trustworthiness. Divine Beauty is reflected, again imperfectly, in the physical order created by God. The world is irradiated with the grandeur of God, a grandeur manifested in the sublime beauty of oceans and mountains, deserts and forests, earth and sky and winds and stars. When we open ourselves to natural beauty, we catch a glimpse of its supremely beautiful Author. Our deiformic connectedness with Beauty calls us forth and we transcend the here-and-now world of "mere" material objects for a universe that shimmers with divinely sourced splendor and glory.

Awe-inspiring experiences of the beauty that saturates the natural world prompted the ancient Greeks to call the universe *kosmos*. The original meaning of *kosmos* suggested an ornament, a thing of great beauty, a decoration. (A drab shred of the word's archaic sense still endures in our "cosmetic.") To the Hellenic eye, reality was the ornament of God, a sparklingly multifaceted gem polished by the divine Artist.

Appreciation of the beauty that suffuses the natural world is also evident in the Hebraic worldview, cropping up as early as the creation account in Genesis. After each of the acts that establish the physical order, God examines his handiwork and declares it *tov*, or "good." But *tov* doesn't merely imply "well made"; it also carries connotations of attractiveness and fairness (as in "a *goodly* maiden"). For both the Greeks and the Hebrews, then, God's creation of the world was an act of *kosmo*-genesis. In breathing the universe into existence, God imbued it with traces of divine Beauty.

The Christian tradition likewise sees God and God's creation as *tov*. Jesus celebrated the beauty of the lilies of the valley (Mt 6:29); Saint Augustine adopted the Platonic notion that ascending orders of worldly beauty guide the human heart to supernatural Beauty; Dionysius the Areopagite claimed that one of the divine names is Beauty; Hilary of Poitiers warmly praised God for the gift of *kosmos*; and Saint Francis was moved to ecstasy by sun and snow. In his treatise *De Potentia*, Thomas Aquinas explicitly interprets the creation account as a sharing of divine Beauty with the physical realm and refers to the latter as *opus ornatus*, a work of ornamentation. The American theologian Jonathan Edwards argued (as we'll examine in some detail later) that natural beauty is the "shadow" or "image" of spiritual or divine Beauty. In recent years, environmentally-conscious Christians have continued the tradition by urging a renewal of our celebration of God/Beauty through reverent stewardship of nature.[2]

The Godluster sees none of this. In strutting his divine power by conquering the natural world, he mutates God's gemlike *kosmos* into "cosmos": a universe of purely material phenomena that can be conceptually gridded, manipulated by human will, and harnessed for human purposes. Cosmos points to nothing beyond itself; it possesses no transcendental qualities. It is simply a vast reservoir of raw material and energy, a collection of "things" whose only value or meaning is to serve the human-God. When the Godluster appropriates *kosmos* in this way and transforms it into cosmos, he necessarily devours beauty. And in devouring beauty, he eliminates— or at least *tries* to eliminate—yet another obstacle to his self-divinization. He stands with Herod on the Mediterranean's shore and commands the wine-dark sea to cease its lovely susurration and do his bidding.

Beauty-eating, like truth-eating, is a demonically desperate tactic to ease ontological anxiety. But like truth-eating, it only aggravates the pain of deiformic separateness. When we denude *kosmos* of its beauty, we condemn ourselves to a world bleakly devoid of God's/Beauty's presence and hence likewise drained of opportunities for transcendence. In this chapter we'll explore how Godlust's devouring of beauty blights the spiritual landscape as well as how we can control its appetite to reestablish the wonder-filled relationship with *kosmos* embraced and celebrated by our ancestors.

Eating Beauty

We saw in chapter 2 that one of the ways the Godluster seeks to establish sovereignty is by making his will the sole standard of truth. One of these "truths" that has proven especially convenient over the centuries is that it's the manifest destiny of humans to subdue the natural world for their own ends.

Doubtlessly this way of thinking has surfaced in each historical period. Herod's lust to conquer the physical realm is a case in point; the legendary King Canute's command of the ocean tides to cease their ebb and flow is another. But it is only in the last three hundred years or so, with the advent of the modern "scientific" age, that the drive to subdue nature has come into its own. Earlier, the urge was sporadic and individualistic; now it's systematic and institutionalized as a primary social value.

Premodern thinking saw the physical realm as God's creation, and consequently acknowledged (even if only half-heartedly at times) that the proper human relationship to nature was stewardship rather than lordship. "The earth is the Lord's and the fullness thereof, the world and those who dwell therein" (Ps 24), and this meant that our role was one of grateful caretaking. But the modern scientific and technological ethos has thrown over this quaint notion. It no longer views humans as divinely appointed stewards, but rather as conquerors and eventual masters of the universe. The first modern conquistador of nature, Francis Bacon (1561–1626), still paid pious if disingenuous lip service to the traditional religious claim that the earth is the Lord's. But the pretension had long been dropped by the time the astronomer Pierre Laplace published his *Exposition du systeme du monde* in 1796. When asked by Napoleon why he'd omitted any mention of God in his book, Laplace confidently replied that he "had no need of the hypothesis."

Laplace did not require the God hypothesis in his account of the universe because the new physicalist worldview he espoused had cleanly amputated the supernatural from the natural. On the surface, this surgery was performed, as Laplace told Napoleon, because science rendered supernatural accounts of the world superfluous. Everything that needed to be explained could be handled quite adequately by quantitative analysis of empirical data. But at a deeper level, God's presence was expunged from the natural world because it threatened human omnipotence. If the natural world is radiated with vestiges of the Divine, if it shimmers with transcendental Presence, then it is beyond the mastery of human intellect and will. Spiritless and value-free physical objects, on the other hand, are eminently manipulable. They pose no significant challenge to the sovereignty of the human-God who wields science as Zeus wielded thunderbolts. As George Herbert Mead exulted, "Humanity was never before so free in dealing with its own environment as it has been since the triumphs of modern science. The ability to look at the world in terms of congeries of physical particles actually has enabled men to determine their environment."[3] Nietzsche as usual was more brutal. Knowledge, he declared, is a "tool of power," and science, "the transformation of nature into concepts for the purpose of mastering nature."[4]

In order for science to transform *kosmos* into cosmos, to eradicate the presence of God's Beauty and reduce the world to a barren landscape comprised of "congeries of physical particles," every recalcitrant trace of the Divine must be slashed and burned. And since beauty is the signal of transcendence through which God is revealed in *kosmos*, beauty must be eaten. Objective beauty can no more be tolerated by the Godluster than objective truth. If beauty exists independently of his will, he is not God. And if he is not God, the universe is not his to master with Nietzsche's "tool of power."

The way Godlust denudes the physical universe of traces of divine Beauty is similar to the way it deals with troublesome vestiges of divine Truth. Beauty becomes a subjective interpretation that we project onto but do not discover in the world. As C. S. Lewis pointed out in *The Abolition of Man*, the beauty-eater contends that whenever we speak of experiences of beauty, what we're really talking about are subjective "feelings," which for purely historical reasons have come to be associated with the word *beauty* or any of its cognates. William Wordsworth, for example, may rhapsodize about the "sublimity" of a waterfall, and thus gesture at a quality he thinks exists objectively. But the Godluster knows what's really going on. When Wordsworth exclaims that "the waterfall is sublime," he's merely describing his own emotional state. What he's really saying is "I have feelings associated in my mind with the word *Sublime*"—or, more to the point, "I have sublime feelings."[5] From where the Godluster stands, Jim Williams was absolutely correct when he maintained that judgments are a function of the beholding eye.

What this means, of course, is that beauty, like truth, is a human invention. Whether it springs from passion or rides on language, as Nietzsche and Rorty respectively said about truth, its ultimate source is the subjective will. The traditional reference point for beauty—God—has been made absent by our ingestion of the beautiful. "Beauty" remains, but dislocated from its proper referent it becomes nothing more than a private matter of taste. And what this boils down to is that we've taken on yet another divine attribute.

Their similarities notwithstanding, a significant distinction exists between truth-eating and beauty-eating that must be kept in mind. Both are ultimately strategies of self-divinization, but their immediate aims differ. The truth-eater's goal is to

acquire omniscience for himself by assuming God's prerogative of defining truth. Truth is the food he craves and stuffs himself with. But the beauty-eater doesn't have an analogous
appetite for the beautiful. He isn't concerned with mastery over
beauty so much as with dominion over nature. Absolute control of the physical realm—omnipotence—is the divine quality
he really craves. It's just that he has to take for himself the prerogative of beauty in order to achieve this goal, because the
presence of divine Beauty in the physical world stands in his
way. Eating beauty is a prelude to devouring *kosmos*. Beauty is
the *apéritif*, nature the main course.

Rape as Destiny

Once our beauty-eating relocates divine Beauty from the
natural to the merely psychological realm, the last line of
defense against the Godluster's invasion of nature falls. Now
the way is laid open for conquest. Francis Bacon bluntly
spelled out the campaign plan for future generations of Godlusting marauders. He likened nature to a "Protean" or whimsical harlot, who first entices humans with her seductive
promises, then coquettishly changes her mind and refuses
her favors. But like all whores, nature "must be taken by the
forelock," thrown on her back, and forcibly ravished.[6] A "man"
ought not "to make scruple of entering and penetrating into
[nature's] holes and corners." Such displays of masculine
resolve both test his mettle and secure for him the longed-for
reward: "For like as a man's disposition is never well known or
proved till he be crossed, nor Proteus ever changed shapes
till he was straitened and held fast, so nature exhibits herself
more clearly under the trials and vexations of [human con-
quest] than when left to herself."[7]

Lest there be any doubt about the propriety of subjecting nature to "trials and vexations," Bacon rather astoundingly invokes the serpent's Edenic promise that humans can be "like unto God" if they "lay hold of [nature] and capture her..., bind her to [their] service and make her [their] slave."[8] What traditionally was viewed as Original Sin is now applauded as the birthright of cosmic conquistadors. It's the job of a God to control nature. Thus humans can become God if they but stretch "the deplorably narrow limits of [their] dominion over the universe" to its "promised bounds".[9] The implication, of course, is that these bounds are limitless.

The sexually ugly tone to Bacon's words captures the beauty-eater's attitude to the physical realm all too well. Nature is no longer a thing of beauty to be admired, wooed, and cherished. It is now a whore whose favors must be taken by force. The conquest of nature, in other words, is likened by Bacon to rape, and his unhappy simile is entirely appropriate. However else rape may be described, it is unarguably a brutal assault that transforms the victim into nothing more than an object to be used and then thrown away. The transformation occurs because the aggressor has imposed on the victim a new definition. He or she is no longer a human being, but rather a thing. Intrinsic value and dignity have been lopped off so that all that remains is a convenient "piece of ass."

In a similarly brutal and vulgar way, the beauty-eater reduces nature to spiritless physicality, stripping it of its divine Beauty and transforming it into an object to be used and tossed. He does this by imposing on the natural order a conceptual grid that absents all traces of divine Beauty that challenge his sovereignty. Recall Nietzsche's earlier insistence that knowledge as a "tool of power" aims to transform nature "into concepts" for the purposes of mastery, as well as my still earlier one that we mutate *kosmos* into cosmos when we straitjacket it in conceptual frameworks that reduce nature to mere physicality. This kind of conceptual redefinition is all too characteristic of Godlust.

As we saw in chapter 2, the truth-eater redefines reality by imposing on it his *own* perspective, his *own* interpretation, thereby taking for himself the divine prerogative of Truth-creation. Now we see a similar mechanism at work in the beauty-eater's campaign against nature. Unable to abide the unconquerably "Protean" presence of natural beauty, he violates it with interpretive schemas that negate it as a signal of transcendence and transform it into a subjective "feeling." Just as the rapist imaginatively recreates a vibrant human being into an impersonal sex toy, so the beauty-eater conceptually remakes Beauty-suffused nature into a Godless thing that can be—that *ought* to be—penetrated and subdued.

Enabling and Making

The twentieth century's most profound insight into how beauty-eaters go about redefining nature in order to absent beauty and conquer the physical realm comes from Martin Heidegger. He calls the techno-scientific grid with which contemporary Godlust disintegrates beauty the *Gestell*, or "frame." The drive to enframe nature isn't merely a theoretical attitude or intellectual stance. It operates at a deeper, more entrenched level as a fundamental response to reality, a way of being that determines our overall "comportment" to the world in which we dwell. Underlying the will to enframe is an understanding of causation as *making* that is particularly appealing to the God-luster because it stamps all creation as utility-laden raw material waiting to be seized and manipulated by humans. We can begin to come to an understanding of the enframer's belligerent notion of causation by first examining its opposite: cause as *enabling*, or *aition*.

For the ancient Greeks, a "cause" or *aition* meant "that to which something else is indebted." Anything that is caused is thereby indebted to, or "owes thanks to," whatever is responsible for enabling it to become what it is: A student is indebted to the teacher who trains his or her mind; children are indebted to the parents who enable them to flourish and grow into adults. To this way of thinking the *agent* of cause, be it teacher or parent, enjoys an especially intimate relationship to that which it enables. It is that generously creative occasion "responsible [for] starting something on its way" to fulfillment or completion. Parents start children on their way to personhood, and teachers start students on their way to self-discovery.[10]

This understanding of cause as *aition* obviously parallels the notion of *aletheia* explored in chapter 2. Clearly, "to cause" something in this sense is to provide an opportunity for its deep meaning to reveal or unconceal. Cause as *aition* is a nurturing, a bringing-forth, a kind of midwifery that invites the object of causation to call out what is inside it, what it truly is. *Aition*, then, is an enabling that is also a revealing.

Although the Greek understanding of causation sounds alien to contemporary ears—a sad indication, Heidegger notes, of just how far we've fallen—in fact it is deeply embedded in the Christian tradition. For the Christian, God is the supreme *Aition*, the divine Enabler who graciously invites forth the world and its inhabitants into existence and sets them on their course. Christians know themselves indebted to God for their very being and, unless poisoned by existential envy, are grateful for the divine gift of life. Moreover, God's creative act of enabling does not lock us into an inflexible program so much as it bestows on us the grace-filled opportunity to develop consciously into what we essentially are: deiform creatures connected to God and on the way to deification. God sets us on our way and guides us, but the direction we finally take is our own free choice: grateful embrace of our connectedness or resentful fixation on our separateness.

But the attitude of enframing has an entirely different understanding of cause; not for it the Greek (much less Christian) notion of *aition*. Enframing works under the assumption that "to cause" is not a gracious act of enablement by which something is invited or called forth to become what it is, but rather a calculated manipulation that forcibly *makes* it into an object of the causer's choosing. The enframer imposes a definition and direction onto an object that ignores what it is and freezes its future into a predetermined path. The enframing parent determines that she wants her child to become, say, a physician. So she defines the child as a future physician and molds him in such a way that all other possibilities for him are negated. The enframing teacher has a preconceived notion of what the "good" student should be, and she forces all her pupils into lockstep conformity to this ideal, rewarding performance that matches her expectation and punishing performance that doesn't. Consequently, Heidegger sees "regulation and securing" as the heart of the causing particular to enframing.[11] If *aition* is best described as *helping* something to reveal its true nature, the causation of enframing is properly defined as *forcing* something to conform to the enframer's own preconceived determination of what it should be.

As we've seen, Heidegger argues that *aition* is a revealing. But he also maintains that the enframer's notion of cause as making is a mode of revealing as well.[12] Given what he's said about its manipulative nature, this claim is startling until we realize that what is "revealed" is simply a reflection of the *Gestell*, or framework, into which the enframer has squeezed reality.

Preconceived definitions and assumptions have a way of incestuously verifying themselves. If I insist upon filtering experience through a conceptual grid that screens out everything except what I want to see, then what is "revealed" naturally matches my expectations. If I'm predisposed to define poverty as a sure sign of laziness, for example, then it's a safe bet that any instance of poverty I encounter in the world will be read through and hence verify my framework assumption. Likewise, if I define persons of color as inferior, my racist enframing of them forces any person of color I meet to match my preconception. I no longer "see" them for who they are. Instead, I "see" them as I've caused/made them to be by shoving them into my bigoted *Gestell*. The "revealing" appropriate to enframing, then, is a predictable self-verification. As Heidegger says, enframing "destinies" revealing.[13]

We've seen that there's a parallel between the revealing of *aition* and the revealing of *aletheia*. Likewise, there's a family resemblance between the "revealing" of enframing and the "revealing" of truth-eating. The truth-eater's appropriation of truth creates and thus "reveals" the pseudoreality spun from his will to power. For Nietzsche, this is the only world there is; for Rorty, it's the only world that matters. Similarly, what enframing "reveals" is also a product of the enframer's will to power. In forcing reality through his "regulating and securing" grid, he fashions it into a thing that both reflects and serves his drive to manipulate and control. And this of course is his goal, for the Godlusting enframer aims to make nature dance to his instrumentalist tune.

Enframing Nature

Now that we've examined Heidegger's claim that the notion of causation appropriate to enframing is *making*, we're ready to explore the specific way in which the beauty-eater enframes the natural realm. (We'll come back to *aition* shortly.) By way of introduction, we can turn to the Russian author Yevgeny Zamyatin's 1920 novel, *We*.

We draws a chilling verbal portrait of a futuristic society locked in mortal combat with nature. The inhabitants of this world dwell in cities completely encased by walls of slick, green glass. Inside the walls are order, precision, law. Whorish nature is controlled down to the smallest detail, and its protean messiness utterly sanitized by gleaming steel, spotless ceramic, and prophylactic brick. Outside the glass walls lies as yet unconquered nature: wild, unpredictable, mysterious, and profoundly terrifying to the people cocooned in their antiseptic cities.

The ultimate goal of *We's* clockwork city-states is to extend technological sovereignty over the entire globe, and this means that nature *outside* the walls will have to be subdued and tamed by science in the same way as nature *inside* the walls. But until that day comes, the high glass fortress, which keeps nature out and precision in, must remain standing.[14]

Zamyatin's portrait is a parable about the beauty-eater's urge to enframe nature. In his city-states of the future, people *literally* "frame" nature with their glass walls. But they also *conceptually* frame nature by transformatively defining it as the hostile Other, an enemy that will dumbly, blindly kill unless first conquered. And the weapon of conquest is the same one that birthed their chrome-like society and built its insulating glass walls in the first place: science. Science, with its ability to divide and conquer through analysis, classification, and manipulation, will tame the beast beyond the walls and harness it for human purposes.

When described in the pages of a futuristic novel, this paranoiac attitude to nature comes across as ludicrous if not outright pathological. But the point Zamyatin wishes to make in his fiction is identical to the point Heidegger makes philosophically: Enframers fear nature and wage war against it. Like the inhabitants of Zamyatin's imaginary cities, they arm themselves with the breastplate of science and the lance of technology. Latter-day Baconians that they are, they see nature as a threat to their conquistador ambitions. It becomes the enemy, and enemies, as Heidegger says, must be "challenged."[15] So they challenge nature by enframing it within the conceptual box of scientific description. They throw it on its back with statistics and measurements, penetrate it with techno-gadgetry, and forcibly bind it with definitions and classifications and categorizations until they've analyzed its mystery away. What's left is exactly what they wanted: a broken-spirited harlot who can be ravished again and again to serve their instrumentalist pleasure. No longer a threat, physical reality becomes merely a standing reserve of riches for the taking.

And in the taking, beauty-eaters cause or *make* nature to "reveal" the exclusively utilitarian essence their enframing has given it. Misty rain forests become reservoirs of timber, awesome mountains depositories of ore, sparkling water an energy source, the blue sky a playground for airplanes and surveillance satellites, the starry heavens the "final frontier." The universe reveals itself as raw material that obediently "stands by," as Heidegger says, until such time as we choose to exploit it.[16] This transformation, moreover, is total. The enframers' *Gestelle* will not tolerate coexistence with rivals.[17]

In a word, the enframer, true to his Baconian roots, uses his techno-scientific grid to make nature into a thing-to-be-raped. What better way to defeat an enemy than through such violent degradation? Rape is only tangentially about pleasure; more essentially, its focus is the seizing and subduing of an other who's seen as a threat. Enframers may argue that what they fear in nature and seek to control with science and technology is the purely physical: disease, earthquakes, droughts, and so on. But this isn't what's really going on. What enrages and terrifies enframers about nature is its sacred dimension, that unquenchable effulgence of divine Beauty that defies their power and mocks their ambition to be God. This is the bottom-line threat to their sovereignty and hence the primary motivation for their manic drive to bend nature to their will. The real foe the beauty-eating enframer battles with his scientific power tools is God; nature is simply the field on which the struggle gets played.

But Heidegger correctly points out that the enframer's attempt to humiliate and master nature leads to his own destruction. Beauty, like *aletheia*, is a shining-forth that calls the soul toward God and deification, and when enframing expunges beauty from the instrumentalist world "revealed" by causing/making, an opportunity for spiritual fulfillment is squandered. Like Herod, modern enframers try to assert their sovereignty by reducing the world to nothing more than standing reserve; sand, sea, and mountains are redefined as just raw materials for fortresses and harbors. But this devastation of beauty only irritates the forlorn sense of separateness and gnawing awareness of inadequacy that ignited their enraged lust in the first place. Eating beauty doesn't give them control of the universe; it hurtles them deeper into the abyss. As Heidegger wisely says,

> The threat to man does not come in the first instance
> from the potentially lethal machines and apparatus of
> technology. The actual threat has already afflicted man
> in his essence. The rule of enframing threatens man with
> the possibility that it could be denied to him to enter
> into a more original revealing and hence experience the
> call of a more primal truth.[18]

Heidegger goes on to ask whether there isn't an alternative response to nature that in fact would allow for a revelatory "shining-forth" of the "primal truth."[19] The answer, of course, is that there is, and it is the response to nature and nature's beauty exemplified by the reverent spirit of *aition* rather than the enframer's coercive spirit of making. It's time now to turn to a consideration of this wonder-filled alternative.

God's Masterpiece

The Bible's approach to the natural world, unlike the enframer's, is a celebration of the "primal truth" of divine Beauty. The earth's seas and sand, mountains and dells, plants and animals; heaven's luminous stars and haunting moon and radiant sun and velvety blue depths: These are all sparkling facets of the gemlike *kosmos* that awaken in the human heart a joyful sense of God's presence.

The biblical insight that God's creation is *kosmos* appears, as we saw at the beginning of this chapter, as early as the Genesis account of creation. God looks upon the newly fashioned universe and sees that it is *tov*. Divine beauty is also reflected in the splendid garden God created for our ancestral parents. The description of Eden in Genesis (2:10–14) evokes exquisite images of finely-wrought art: a land harmoniously intersected by four rivers and bounded by sparkling gold and glittering bedellium and onyx.

Surely one of the horrors of the expulsion was the loss of such beauty. Equally unsettling is the fact that the human relationship to nature seems to have shifted after the Edenic fall. Before, the earth had been a thing of splendor that delighted Adam and Eve. Afterwards, their perception was more instrumentalist; earth became a thing from which to wrest a precarious living (Gn 3:23). God's beauty was still present in nature; creation remained *tov*. But the worm of Godlust had already begun to tarnish human appreciation of it.

In spite of the Edenic Fall and its corruption of our original wonderment at nature, the ancient Hebrews still knew the earth to be the Lord's, not just in the sense of ownership but more significantly in the sense that beauty, God's signature, is everywhere upon it. The supreme *Tov* actively indwells the *tov* creation: "...I will make my abode among you..." (Lv 26:11); "...the Lord your God is he who is God in heaven above *and* on earth beneath" (Jos 2:11). God's ongoing presence in the world is manifested through the splendor, radiance, sublimity, and harmony—in other words, through the sheer beauty—of nature. The Lord God created a "fair land" (Dt 8:7) because God himself is "a crown of glory" and a "diadem of beauty" (Is 28:5; cf. Ps 104:1–4). Beauty shines forth even in those terrible moments when divine wrath blackens the heavens. It is the rainbow, after all, a phenomenon of incredible beauty and delicacy, which God uses in the wake of the Great Flood to symbolize the renewed covenant between himself and humankind (Gn 9:12).

Some of the most lyrical passages in the Old Testament are celebrations of the beauty that enduringly pervades nature.

Godlust

One of King David's earliest recorded hymns (1 Chr 16:9,12) exuberantly praises the creative genius of the divine Artist:

> Sing to him, sing praises to him,
>> tell of all his wonderful works!
>> …Remember the wonderful works he has done,
>> the wonders he wrought!

The "wonderful works" David celebrates are legion. Some take our breath away by the majestic intensity of their beauty. The author of Job, for example, is awed by the God/Beauty who

> stretched out the heavens…,
> made the Bear and Orion,
>> the Pleiades and the chambers of the south;
> who does great things beyond understanding,
>> and marvelous things without number. (Jb 9: 8, 9–10)

But the same author also recognizes that divine Beauty's signals of transcendence are found even in those natural objects we so take for granted that we scarcely notice them for the signals of transcendence they are. Beauty shines forth everywhere. The entire *kosmos* proclaims it. All we need do is open our hearts to its ubiquitous presence:

> Ask the beasts, and they will teach you;
>> the birds of the air, and they will tell you;
> or the plants of the earth, and they will teach you;
>> and the fish of the sea will declare to you. (Jb 12:7–8)

Jesus famously expresses this same insight when he urges his listeners to slow down and take time to notice the astounding beauty of commonplace things like lilies of the field and birds of the air (Mt 6:25–34).

Many of the psalms likewise exalt the gift of beauty that God has bestowed on the natural order. The psalmist looks at the world and is overwhelmed with its magnificence. Each created thing reflects the beauty of the Lord; its palpable presence stretches from horizon to horizon. "The heavens are telling the glory of God; and the firmament proclaims his handiwork" (Ps 19). The beauty that saturates the physical realm not only invites celebratory responses of wonderment and awe from humans. It's also a cause of grateful rejoicing by God-adorned nature herself. "Let the earth rejoice; let the many coastlands be glad!" (Ps 97); "Make a joyful noise to the Lord, all the earth; break forth into joyous song and sing praises!" (Ps 98); "Praise God, sun and moon, praise him, all you shining stars! Praise him, you highest heavens, and you waters above the heavens!" (Ps 148). This wonderful intuition that nature herself celebrates the gift of God/Beauty surely is part of what Paul was getting at when he wrote that all creation longs for the redemptive moment when its divine radiance and glory will become manifest to the human heart (i.e., Rom 8:19–23).

What's especially noteworthy about the biblical understanding of beauty is that it anticipates and cautions against the techno-scientific enframer's drive to eat beauty and "reveal" nature as standing reserve. The Book of Job is a case in point. In one of his soliloquies (28:1–4, 9–11), Job ruminates on the post-Edenic tendency of humans to see the earth as nothing more than exploitable raw material.

> Surely there is a mine for silver,
> > and a place for gold which [humans] refine.
> Iron is taken out of the earth,
> > and copper is smelted from the ore.
> Men put an end to darkness,
> > and search out to the farthest bound
> > the ore in gloom and deep darkness....

Man puts his hand to the flinty rock,
   and overturns mountains by the roots.
He cuts out channels in the rocks,
   and his eye sees every precious thing.
He binds up the streams so that they do not trickle,
   and the thing that is hid he brings forth to light.

Thus do humans seek to redefine nature as standing reserve and penetrate its rich darkness. But if they do so, Job plaintively asks, "Where shall wisdom be found?" (28:12). In posing this question, Job expresses the same fear of enframing voiced centuries later by Heidegger. The Hebrew word translated here as "wisdom" can also be rendered as "artistic creativity" or "beauty-making"; in Exodus 36:11, for example, the artisans who skillfully build the tabernacle are referred to as "wise" men. Job's question clearly intends this meaning. In effect, it asks this: If humans treat the earth as mere raw material, what then of beauty? What then of God? But in spite of his concern, Job remains confident that wisdom/beauty is ultimately untouchable by enframing (12:11). Attempts to quantify the natural and reduce the wisdom/beauty that imbues it to physical status cannot succeed in the long run. Humans may destroy themselves in the undertaking, but not divine Beauty.

The biblical message is clear: Nature—*kosmos*—is a divine masterpiece properly cherished rather than exploited. The Lord's earth remains *tov* even if our Godlust blinds us to its beauty. God, as the Renaissance painter Vasari said, is the first and best Artist.[20]

God *the* Masterpiece

What can we say about this divine Wisdom/Beauty that permeates the world with dazzling light, is the occasion for jubilant celebration even by nature herself, and is present in but not reducible to the physical order?

Thomas Aquinas argued that beauty has three distinctive features: *integritas sive perfectio*, "integrity or wholeness"; *debita proportio sive consonantia*, "right proportion or harmony"; and *claritas*, "radiance."[21] Something is beautiful when its individual parts or components harmonize with one another to form a radiant whole. This characterization of beauty is not original to Thomas. Earlier Western thinkers, from Plato through Plotinus and Augustine, likewise understood beauty as wholeness, harmony, and radiance.[22]

If God is the source of beauty in the natural order and if natural beauty possesses wholeness, harmony, and radiance, then these three qualities must be supremely present in God. God isn't just the First Artist, Creator of the *kosmic* masterpiece. God is also *the* masterpiece, Beauty itself.

Obviously this claim needs unpacking. In order to do that, we may turn to the early American theologian Jonathan Edwards (1703–58). Few Christian thinkers have been more struck by natural beauty than Edwards; none have so systematically explored beauty as a signal of transcendence—or what Edwards preferred to call an "image" or "shadow" of the divine. "God," says Edwards, "is distinguished . . . chiefly by his divine beauty," and the "beauty of the world is a communication of God's beauty."[23] Like Thomas, Edwards believes that the "beauty of the world" is expressed in wholeness, harmony, and radiance. The divine correlates of these three features he understands as Being, Love, and Holiness: Natural beauty's wholeness is a shadow of God's Being, its harmony a shadow of God's Love, and its radiance a shadow of God's Holiness. The masterpiece reflects *the* Masterpiece; beauty reflects Beauty.

Wholeness/Being. An object is beautiful, said Thomas, when it displays "integrity" or "wholeness." This suggests that a beautiful thing, however complex or multifaceted it may be, possesses a form that bestows upon it an identity of its own and makes it what it is. Form is the necessary condition for a thing's very being as well as its integrity or completeness—its "wholeness." The close relationship between beauty and formal wholeness is especially obvious in Latin; one of the words for beauty, *formositas*, is derived from the adjective *formosus*, or "well-formed."

Edwards agrees that to be is necessarily to possess a form that imparts integrity and identity, and that the beauty of an object is proportionate to its degree of unified being or formal wholeness. But the being of natural objects—and, indeed, the being of the entire universe—is borrowed, emanating from God, the "Being of beings." Consequently, the being or wholeness of the natural world is always and everywhere radically dependent upon the God who is perfect Wholeness, absolute Form. The closer a created object's being approximates divine Being, the more complete or perfect is that object's form: "A being . . . is the more excellent because [it] partakes more of Being."[24] All created objects participate in varying degrees in the Being of beings, and it is this participation that imparts *formositas* to them. Natural beauty, then, is the "diffused reflection" of that Being who is

> the foundation and fountain of all being and all beauty;
> from whom all is perfectly derived, and on whom all is
> most absolutely and perfectly dependent; of whom and
> through whom, and to whom is all being and perfection;
> and whose being and beauty is as it were the sum and
> comprehension of all existence and excellence.[25]

If beauty is connected to form, and if form in turn is a reflection of divine Being, it follows that when we heed the call of beauty in the physical realm, what we really harken to is the supreme Beauty of divine Being. We sense the perfect Being/perfect Beauty of God behind and within the form of natural objects. This is the *integritas* to which our deiform natures connect us and for which our hearts yearn. The beauty-eating enframer is wrong; it is not the techno-scientific grid that bestows form on the universe. The natural order already possesses form, a shadow of the Being who is Beauty itself.

Harmony/Love. Thomas said that an object is beautiful if it possesses "right proportion" or "harmony"—that is, if its various parts are in proper relation to one another. Harmony is a feature of beauty that obviously complements form; wholeness is possible only if there is coherence or harmony among an object's parts. Thus the beauty/being of a flower, for example, is dependent on the harmonious arrangement of its texture, hues, and shape into a unified whole. As Edwards says, "discord and dissent" are incompatible with beauty. Consequently,

> the beauty of [natural objects] is, when one part has such consonant proportion with the rest as represents a general agreeing and consenting together.... Therein consists the beauty of figures..., and the beauty of the body, and of the features of the face.[26]

Harmony in the natural order, just like form, ultimately derives from God. Because divine Being is perfect in every way, there is no discord or dissent among its "parts." Edwards invokes trinitarian imagery to get across his meaning. The three divine hypostases of the Trinity, who together constitute divine Being, are in perfect harmony or proportion with one another, analogous to the way well-tempered musical notes are proportionately related. *Consonantia* or "harmony" in fact literally means a "sounding together" of individual notes such that their diversity constitutes a melodious unity. So it is with God: the interplay in divine Being between Father, Son, and Holy Spirit is a perfect *consonantia*.

Edwards argues that natural beauty reflects divine harmony because all created beings "sweetly consent" to, or harmonize with, the Being who is their source. Since natural objects depend for their existence on God and thus reflect God's Being, they "concord" with God in right or proper proportion. This *consonantia* between Creator and creation is reflected at every level of reality, imparting a "general agreeing and consenting together" to the entire *kosmos*. The world harmonizes with God, natural objects in the world harmonize with other natural objects, and the individual parts of each natural object harmonize with one another. Everywhere creation "sweetly consents" to God.[27]

We saw earlier that Edwards considers Being as the divine correlate of form in the natural realm. He now tells us that the harmony we discern in natural beauty is a reflection of the binding power of divine Love. Love among the persons of the Trinity is what enables them to "sound together." God's Love for creation is the bind that harmonizes the *kosmos* with the Creator and the parts of the *kosmos* with one another. "When one thing sweetly harmonizes with another," Edwards says, "as the notes in music, the notes are so conformed and have such proportion one to another that they seem to have respect one to another, *as if they loved one another.*"[28]

It follows that harmonious "beauties of nature" in fact "are really emanations or shadows" of the divine Love that holds

the universe together. That Love, claims Edwards, is epitomized in Jesus the Christ. Jesus *is* Love, the great Harmonizer
who woos reality into sweet mutual consent with God. Consequently, when we observe harmony in nature, we are really
intuiting the Beauty of Christ:

> When we are delighted with flowery meadows and gen-
> tle breezes of wind, we may consider that we only see
> the emanations of the sweet benevolence of Jesus
> Christ; when we behold the fragrant rose and lily, we see
> his love and purity. So the green trees and fields, and
> singing of birds, are the emanations of his infinite joy
> and benignity; the easiness and naturalness of trees and
> vines [are] shadows of his infinite beauty and loveliness;
> the crystal rivers and murmuring streams are the foot-
> steps of his sweet grace and bounty.[29]

For Edwards, then, the beauty of the natural world not only
awakens us to a sense of divine Being. It also leads us to an
experience of the divine Love that sustains all creation. The
beautifully harmonious fabric of existence is threaded
throughout with divine Love. And Love resists enframing's
divide-and-conquer strategy to reduce *kosmos* to cosmos.

Radiance/Holiness. According to Thomas, a beautiful
object projects *claritas*, or radiance. "Light," "radiance," "illu-
mination": These were favorite metaphors with which the Hel-
lenes and medievalists attempted to express a sudden inrush
of deep meaning into the human heart and mind. Beautiful
objects are purveyors of such meaning. When we encounter
them, they impart insight to us that lightens our darkness and
fills us with a sense of our connectedness to something
greater than ourselves. This encounter with deep meaning, so
overwhelming that words can scarcely utter it, is at the heart

of an "aesthetic" experience. As we saw in chapter 2, it's also the essence of *aletheia's* revelation of Mystery.

The radiance of beautiful objects, then, is an unconcealment of God. What specifically is unconcealed is divine *Claritas*, the never-diminishing radiance—or, as Edwards says, the "Holiness"—of the Being of beings. When we run up against the radiance of natural beauty, we experience a "shadow" of its divine correlate, Holiness.

Edwards regards Holiness as God's most elemental quality. "Holy, holy, holy Lord, God of power and might." Holiness is the shining-forth of divine majesty and glory. Even more than Love, Edwards asserts, Holiness is the sacred essence of God. The divine Wholeness who imparts form to created beings and whose Love harmonizes the entire natural order is first and foremost transcendent Holiness, a Being of effulgent splendor who transfigures reality with shimmering radiance. As Edwards says, "That beauteous light with which the world is filled in a clear day is a lively shadow of [God's] spotless holiness."[30] Wherever we are, we stand on sacred ground.

We especially notice the radiant Holiness that permeates the natural order in those moments of sublimity that C. S. Lewis's beauty-eaters so casually dismiss as mere subjective moods. A majestic waterfall or a thunderstorm at sea unconceal for us a hint of the unspeakably mysterious glory of Holy Being. Such encounters can be as terrifying as they are profoundly fulfilling. The overwhelming beauty of Holiness blows us out of the here-and-now, and the explosion inevitably ignites the God-desire that lies at the core of our being. But it also reveals to us our utter insignificance in the face of divine majesty. For some of us, this recognition of total dependency on God only magnifies our gratitude and adoration for the Being who enables our being. But the humbling beauty of

Holiness is yet another thorn in the enframer's flesh, and his frantic beauty-eating is an attempt to pluck it out. If ever there was a quality that cannot be erased, however, it is Holiness. Trying to enframe it out of existence is as futile as attempting to quench the sun with a garden hose.

Returning to Beauty

When we devour beauty to strip God's presence from nature, we rob ourselves of opportunities for transcendence because, as Edwards has helped us see, we gut the world of its traces of divine Being, Love, and Holiness. This reduction of *kosmos* to starkly spiritless cosmos leaves us, Heidegger says, "homeless."[31] Our promised haven, our intended home, is God. In succumbing to Godlust, we wayward sons and daughters forsake our hearths to roam in the wilderness without true direction or genuine purpose. The demonic has no permanent abode; it flits from one place to another, forever driven by its restless craving.

Like the prodigal son in scripture, however, we can return home. The enframing by which we foolishly hope to master creation and assume divinity need not orphan us. We can awaken to *kosmos* and thereby discover both God and our own true selves.

Edwards pointed us homewards when he spoke of the way nature "sweetly consents" to the divine Beauty that birthed it. There is a natural concordance between physical and spiritual beauty, such that the former "lovingly assents" to the latter. To escape Godlust, we must consciously follow nature's lead by cultivating a sweet "consent, propensity, and union of heart to Being in general."[32] Instead of enframing nature as a spiritless Other to be challenged and defeated, we need to recognize it as the divinely harmonious thing it is. Instead of seizing and making/causing nature to serve our instrumentalist purposes, we must learn to nurture and cherish its signal of transcendent Holiness. Our deiform natures already predispose us in this direction. Like all created things, we are innately connected to the divine Source. The trick is to assent to that connectedness.

Sweetly consenting to the beauty of Being implies neither a passive hands-off policy toward nature nor a fatalistic endurance of those natural phenomena that pose genuine risks to our physical well-being. There's no suggestion here that we burn our science books or resign ourselves to the ravages of diseases and disasters. Rather, the point is that we rethink science to transform it from a power tool that reveals and coerces cosmos to a vehicle for grateful and celebratory communion with *kosmos*. This means that we heed the call (*kaleo*) of beauty (*kalon*) to cooperate rather than manipulate, to partake of beautiful Being rather than to erase it through enframing, to aim for intimacy instead of bellicosity. It means, in short, returning to the stewardship of nature God originally intended us for.

Consenting to God's beauty, then, is a two-step movement. First, we open ourselves to its call by cultivating a sensitivity to what the British priest and poet Gerard Manley Hopkins (1844–89) referred to as nature's "inscape." Second, we exercise stewardship by forsaking our enframed understanding of cause as "making" and returning to a relationship with nature guided instead by "enabling," or *aition*.

Awakening to Inscape. Enframers trap themselves in the *Gestelle* they construct, thereby closing themselves off to reality as the God-saturated thing it is and dwelling instead in the instrumentalist reality their making/causing has "revealed."

The first step in awakening to the call of beauty is the cultivation of an attitude toward our techno-scientific grids very much like the Ignatian *indiferençia* to self explored in chapter 2. This consists at least in the steady recognition that our attempts to scientifically define and classify nature are radically provisional and always run the risk of obfuscating rather than revealing Being. Admitting the artificiality of such frames opens the way for moving beyond them to a discernment of the underlying essence of nature, which, as we've seen, is Beauty. It need not mean that we forsake our efforts to understand and use physical nature, but it does entail that we gratefully, humbly, and reverentially acknowledge its spiritual depth.

Gerard Manley Hopkins was well aware of beauty-eating's lust to enframe nature in exclusively utilitarian categories. In one of his finest poems he laments that what once was *kosmos* has been perversely

> ...seared with trade; bleared, smeared with toil;
> And wears man's smudge and shares man's smell: the soil
> Is bare now, nor can foot feel, being shod.

But "for all this," Hopkins continues,

> nature is never spent;
> There lives the dearest freshness deep down things....[33]

It is that deep-down freshness, that sacred vitality and holy presence "bleared" by enframing's absenting of divine Beauty, that we must recover. Hopkins calls it the "inscape."

The inscape of a natural object—and by implication, of the entire natural order as well—is the beneath-the-surface "oneness" that holds the object's components in a state of harmony. Casual observers of nature tend to focus on "outscaped" sense-impressions such as color, texture, aroma or taste, and ignore the inscape upon which they ride. Similarly, enframers blind themselves to the inscape because they've arrogantly imposed a conceptual outscape that negates it. But when we go beyond casual observation, or when we cultivate *indiferençia* long enough to step back from our egoistic redefinition of nature as standing reserve, we open ourselves to the possibility of experiencing the world as it really is. And when we do this, the inscaped oneness that undergirds and radiates from all created things flows forth. What Thomas called wholeness, harmony, and radiance, then, is what Hopkins calls oneness. When we attune to it, we experience an alethic revelation of the Being, Love, and Holiness that lie at the heart of creation. We discern the divine Beauty of *kosmos*.

Hopkins' letters and journals record several occasions in which the inscape revealed itself to him. He speaks, for example, of the experience of "seeing freshly" the wholeness/Being of bleached tufts of grass standing upright in a frozen field. He marvels at their form, and rejoices that his "eye," or sensitivity to the spiritual Beauty that imbues physical objects, is "still growing."[34] Elsewhere he speaks of similar revelatory moments when gazing upon tree twigs or bluebells; to experience them as they truly are, unfiltered through artificial *Gestelle*, is to intuit the shimmering radiance/Holiness of the Lord.[35] And in the most dramatic of all his inscaping experiences, Hopkins is awed by harmony/Love revealed in a sunset. Prior to this moment of unconcealment, he tells us, he'd always visually separated the setting sun from the objects its rays illuminated, neatly placing each in their proper conceptual boxes. "But today," he marvels, "I inscaped them together," and the whole unveiled itself "as it is": a seamlessly unified yet "active and tossing" whole.[36] Form, harmony, light; Being, Love, Holiness: Such is the unconcealment that occurs when we allow the natural order out of our boxes and invite its inscaped "oneness" to come forth. It's little wonder that in another of his poems Hopkins thanks God for the world's thousands of sweetly consenting "dappled things":

> For skies of couple-colour as a brinded cow;
>> For rose-moles in all stipple upon trout that swim;
> Fresh-firecoal chestnut-falls; finches' wings;
>> Landscape plotted and pieced—fold, fallow, and plough.

Beneath all the marvelous complexity of the world is a "fathering-forth" of that "whose beauty is past change": God.[37] When we attune ourselves to the inscape of creation, we rediscover the call of that beauteous fathering-forth. And when this happens, beauty-eating's lust to master nature has no choice but to give way to grateful wonderment and adoration.

Enabling. As Hopkins discovered, an experience of the shimmering inscape that underlies and sustains the world's physical outscape fundamentally changes our response to the created order. After the revelation of inscape, we no longer view the world as spiritless standing reserve whose only function is to gratify our instrumentalist ambitions. Nature now unconceals as a wondrous thing of divinely appointed beauty, a God-saturated *kosmos*, an emanation of divine Being (form), Love (harmony), and Holiness (radiance). Inevitably, our relationship to it changes from the forcible *making* characteristic of enframing to the *enabling* of stewardship.

The Godluster longs to become the God-who-devours, and he eats beauty in order to force nature to do his bidding. The God-desirer's goal, on the other hand, is to grow into God, to become more and more Godlike in spirit and comportment until, with God's grace, she reaches the divine interpenetration of deification.

We've already seen in this chapter that God is the great Enabler who "causes" by generously inviting forth the essence of every created thing and lovingly setting it on its way. If we would imitate God, we too must become enablers. In our case, what we enable is the unimpeded shining of the inscape embedded within the natural order. To borrow a phrase from Heidegger, we must become "shepherds" of beauty who nurture and love it into a full blossoming-forth.[38]

Beauty's call for us to be enablers is yet another example of the universal harmony or sweet concordance that so impressed Jonathan Edwards. Just as God reaches out to us through the signals of divine Beauty found in nature, so we reach out to God when we recognize and embrace them. Just as those revealings enable us to call to the surface that which we essentially are—creatures made by and for God—so we enable the revealings to unconceal by opening ourselves to them. Beauty is and endures, because God is and endures; but the *revealing* of beauty depends, after all, on the existence of subjects who are receptive to the revealing. When we cultivate this receptivity, we invite forth and set on its way the inscape, the beautiful essence, of the natural realm. Instead of *making* nature "reveal" as spiritless standing reserve, we become occasions that *enable* nature to reveal what it genuinely is. This is the heart of what it means to be a steward or shepherd.

More specifically, stewardship of nature/beauty involves two interrelated responses. The first is humble gratitude; the second is joyful service.

A good steward knows herself indebted to the inscaped traces of divine Beauty in the world because the revealings of those traces unconceal for her both the radiant glory of God and her own essential connectedness with God. Consequently, she is profoundly grateful. At the same time, however, she also recognizes her utter inability to seize and devour either beauty or nature, and this reminds her of the self's intrinsic mediocrity (recall the discussion in chapter 2) as well as her radical indebtedness to God. Thus her gratitude for the revealing of divine Beauty is coupled with a proper sense of her own insignificance in the face of it. The relentless egoism of Godlust falls away, and she sees herself in all her fragile nakedness. But this newly discovered humility, far from seeding the destructive resentment of existential envy, only increases the steward's gratitude for the gift of beauty: The less she knows herself to have, the more she appreciates what she's been given.

Humble gratitude for the revealing of inscaped beauty creates in the steward a great desire to be worthy of the gift, and she joyfully enters into its service. As we've already seen, such service entails an attitude of enabling or shepherding natural beauty rather than devouring and enframing it. More specifically, the steward's gratitude prompts her to serve divine Beauty by nurturing and cherishing nature and by helping others to awaken to its call.

Nurturing and cherishing nature first and foremost means reverencing its being as an extension of God's Being, honoring it for the Holiness that it radiates, and loving it for the sake of the divine Love that holds all creation together. Nothing in nature is worthy of contempt; nothing in nature ought to be squandered or poisoned or enframed into mere standing reserve. As I said earlier, this doesn't mean that we turn our backs on science and technology, but rather that we rethink their assumptions, methods, and goals in light of what the experience of Beauty has revealed about the world in which we dwell. Science must become friendly and technology green so that they are vehicles which enable nature to flourish rather than tools of power for its exploitation. Instead of raping nature like Baconian conquistadors and leaving in our wake extinct species, dead farmland, mistreated animals, and befouled water and air, we must act, both as individuals and as policy makers, to guarantee that the revealings of divine Beauty in nature can come forth. When we do so, we not only serve/enable the planet. We also serve/enable God.

Stewards are called to both shepherd beauty and enable others to experience the revealing of inscaped Beauty and thereby become enablers themselves. This is best done by example. The good steward brings to light the Being, Love, and Holiness of nature by comporting herself in "sweet consent" to them. Experiencing both her own and nature's utter dependence on God's Being, she helps others to know the grateful joy such a gift brings her. Feeling herself an integral part of the *kosmic* harmony sounded by divine Love, she expresses that love in her life by selflessly midwiving the beauty in nature as well as in humans. Awed by the presence of Holiness, she strives to awaken others to its wonderment as well. In short, a good steward becomes the conduit through which God's Being, Love, and Holiness can flow. She cannot be the master of Beauty. But she can become beautiful by allowing Beauty to master her.

The ancient Romans looked upon the first followers of Jesus and exclaimed: "How these Christians love one another!" Contemporary stewards/enablers should so live the Beauty of God that their peers look at them and exclaim: "How these Christians love creation!" For the earth is the Lord's. The palace-fortresses of Masada and Herodium have crumbled atop their mountains, and the wine-dark sea and white sands have reclaimed the harbor at Caesarea Maritima. But the Beauty of God endures.

Chapter Four

Godlust and the Good

*Things are beginning to shape up. It is a long
time since anyone stole the park benches or
murdered the swans. There are children in
this province who have never seen a louse,
shopkeepers who have never handled a
counterfeit coin, women of forty who have
never hidden in a ditch except for fun. Yes,
in twenty years I have managed to do a little.*

Herod

No one is good but God alone.

Mark 10:18

Saving Civilization

The Serpent is cunning. He knows that the best way to
drive us ruinously from deep to deeper is to play up to our
most cherished ideals and principles. Let the hideous worm

that twists in our hearts show its true colors, and all but the most callous Godlusters will recoil in shame and horror. But drape the worm's poisonous intentions in high-minded talk about human betterment and social reform, and even Original Sin palatably comes across as altruism.

The Adversary, in short, is a good propagandist. He realizes that heavy-handed Faustian bribes that play up to our basest passions are generally off-putting. Much more effective is the sly insinuation that those passions in fact are idealistic impulses to serve others. Thus the truth-eater often thinks that her demolition of objective truth liberates humans from hurtful dogmatism, and the beauty-eater typically believes that his assault on nature is a crusade to improve the quality of life. But the sheer arrogance of their underlying pretensions of omniscience and omnipotence reveals what's really going on. Regardless of how truth-eaters and beauty-eaters may sugarcoat their motives, what drives them is the lust to be God.

Nowhere is the sin of Godlust more cunningly disguised than in good-eating. When the Godluster devours the Good, he sets himself up as the supreme lawmaker and final judge of what's good and what's evil. He sees himself as an idealistic reformer, a crusader for justice and progress and prosperity, a prophet of the utopian golden age. But this is demonic deception. Lurking underneath his facade of altruism is the incessant craving to wield absolute moral dominion over humans. If the truth-eater strives for Godhood by subjectivizing truth and the beauty-eater divinizes himself by forcibly squeezing nature through his instrumentalist *Gestelle*, the good-eater seeks to become God by controlling and manipulating people—but always, of course, for their "own good."

We may look to Herod once more for an illustration of good-eating. This time the Herod to whom we turn comes neither from Josephus nor medieval mystery plays, but from W. H. Auden's haunting Christmas oratorio "For the Time Being." In it, Auden takes a fresh look at an old character. His Herod isn't a bloodthirsty lunatic or an unpredictable megalomaniac. Instead, he's a distressingly contemporary bureaucrat, an administrative paper pusher who does what he thinks he must to usher in the perfect society, or what he refers to as the "Rational Life." Sometimes this means he must commit evil for the sake of doing "good." Herod doesn't relish the prospect, and occasionally is even disturbed by its necessity. But he's willing to sacrifice scruples to force through his imperious vision of the good.

That vision is of a society which runs with clockwork or "rational" perfection. Persons do what they're supposed to do; they obey the laws Herod ordains for their own well-being and conform to the values he designates as absolute standards. If heeded, Herod's visionary decrees will inaugurate an unblemished era of individual happiness and social progress. They will create Utopia, the heavenly city. And Herod, the omnibenevolent architect of this new paradise, of course will rule over it—which means that he will be God.

The problem is that Herod's wayward and "irrational" subjects have other ideas. They fight him every inch of the way, moronically resisting his noble plans to reform them. "How can I expect the masses to be sensible?" he laments.[1] True, Herod's backbreaking labor to achieve the good has had some success; "the darkness," he reflects, "has been pushed back a few inches." He knows, however, that the task calls for constant vigilance. "[W]hat, after all, is the whole Empire, with its few thousand square miles on which it is possible to lead the Rational Life, but a tiny patch of light compared with those immense areas of barbaric night that surround it on all sides... ?"[2]

But such moments of gloomy frustration are quickly thrown off. Continuously reenergized by his vision of the good, valiant Herod holds the line, tirelessly working to preserve the boundaries that keep the encircling darkness of irrationality at bay and mercilessly weeding those shadowy patches that crop up within his kingdom's borders. Anything that hampers progress by deflecting human energy away "from its normal and wholesome outlet" of obedience to Herod's moral will must be eradicated.[3]

Now, however, the greatest threat of all to the Rational Life has arrived on the scene. There is a distressing rumor that God has been born in a tiny village, a God who brings a message of love and compassion and freedom instead of subservience to Herodian law. There will be no holding back the darkness if this rumor spreads among the gullible masses. It is capable of "diseasing the whole Empire" with its wild promise of spiritual liberation and self-discovery. "Justice"—the rule of Herodian law—"Justice will be replaced by Pity as the cardinal human virtue."[4] And when this happens, the bottom drops out. Herod can deal with resentful mutterings or even angry rebellion against his vision of the good. But this new gospel is a powder keg that threatens to demolish everything he's labored to build.

Herod the bureaucrat, Herod the administrator, has stayed up nights perusing the government reports. He's consulted his policy makers and security advisors, studied the statistics, memorized the economic projections. Nothwithstanding the occasional setback, everything is still more or less on course. The kingdom of Herod-the-God is at hand, the golden age of reform just around the corner—and it "must be saved," Herod ominously resolves, "even if this means sending for the military."[5] For the good of society, for the good of the people, he will rescue them from themselves. If they're too shortsighted to know what's in their best interests, they must be made to understand. If they won't be rationally persuaded, then the sword must force them to see the light. After all, Herod's vision is for *their* own good; the only thing he wants is *their* good. So he will neutralize this latest threat to the Rational Life by slaughtering every infant in Bethlehem. An unfortunate necessity, perhaps, but a necessity nonetheless: No challenger of Herod's divinity must be allowed to disrupt the march toward Utopia. And if his people—the ungrateful curs!—vilify him for his efforts, so be it. He knows that his heart is pure.

> I've worked like a slave. Ask anyone you like. I read all official dispatches without skipping. I've taken elocution lessons. I've hardly ever taken bribes.... I've tried to be good. I brush my teeth every night. I haven't had sex for a month.... I want everyone to be happy.[6]

Auden's King Herod is a chilling example of the complex nature of good-eating. On the one hand, we must take Herod at his word. His dedication is sincere. He truly wants to stamp out the "darkness" that threatens to subvert the Rational Life. He honestly wishes everyone's happiness. But on the other hand, the values he seeks to impose on his subjects are his own inventions. In pressing them, he tolerates no competition; *his* way is the only right way, *his* will the final arbiter of good and evil, *his* vision of the good life the sole absolute. He and he alone holds the secret to social perfection and individual happiness: Obey his laws and salvation is at hand. So it's only proper that the people bend to his will. If they resist his attempts to make them good, he'll do whatever it takes to break their obduracy. He, Herod the savior, will make them conform to the values he's decreed for them. It's an unpleasant task, but one he conscientiously assumes, because such is the duty of a Messiah. For make no mistake about it: In taking upon himself the authority to lay down the law about how people ought to live and what they ought to value, Herod has eaten the Good and thereby crowned himself the saving God. This is the real meaning of his or any other good-eater's "altruism."

Eating the Good

Good-eating is the culminating moment in the Godluster's theophagic campaign to escape ontological anxiety. Truth-eaters take the first step when they seize God's prerogative to determine truth and meaning. Beauty-eaters continue the process by enframing divine Beauty out of the natural world to bend it to their divine will. Good-eaters cap off the campaign by nudging out God as the ultimate standard of the Good. With this final onslaught against the divine Other whose very Being they resentfully envy, Godlusters add messianic omnibenevolence to their already usurped qualities of omniscience and omnipotence.

As we'll see later in this chapter, our deiform nature calls us to embrace and imitate divine Goodness. Jesus reminded us (Mt 19:17; Mk 10:18; Lk 18:19) that God alone is absolutely Good; consequently, God is always the supreme normative standard by which we ought to measure ourselves. But this is a dependency the resentful good-eater will not accept because it too uncomfortably reminds him that he lacks Godly self-sufficiency. So like his spiritual ancestor Herod, he rebels by proclaiming his own will the final source of value. Once again God is made an absent referent. In other words, that to which "Good" traditionally pointed—God—is absented by the good-eater's taking for himself the authoritative wisdom to define and legislate the Good. Goodness is no longer objective, much less a signal that points beyond itself to a transcendent Reality. Now it's a reflection of the human-God's will.

Three points need to be kept in mind about the nature of good-eating. The first is that it ought not to be interpreted as mere ethical subjectivism. True, there is a certain intersection between the two positions. Both the good-eater and the ethical subjectivist, for example, measure themselves in terms of how indomitably they resolve not to be bound by any values other than the ones their choices absolutize. Conformity to social mores or traditional values—much less atavistic scriptural codes of conduct—isn't for the likes of them. They see such conformity as disgraceful subservience born of cowardice or lack of vision. Both the good-eater and the ethical subjectivist consider themselves morally superior to any external criteria of behavior. Each is his own standard. Each is normatively self-determined, morally *causa sui*.

They part ways, however, in this regard: Whereas the ethical subjectivist is perfectly willing to allow others the same normative autonomy she demands for herself, the good-eater is not. The ethical subjectivist is consistent in her reduction of values to individual whim. But the good-eater absolutizes his own moral will as *the* standard for how everyone else ought to behave. He alone has the strength of will to liberate himself from the petty value systems of religion or society; he alone enjoys an untarnished vantage point. Consequently, his normative wisdom is authoritative. Like Herod, he knows how to push back the darkness and usher in the heavenly kingdom. All other humans, lacking as they do his ethical acumen, properly ought to listen and obey.

In the second place, it's also an error to read the good-eater as a cynically self-serving Machiavellian or Nietzschean "great man." Once again, though, there is some overlap. Machiavelli and Nietzsche believed, for example, that what distinguishes "great men" from the hoi polloi is their possession of the courage and iron will to walk their own ways and carve out their own values. The good-eater believes this as well. Moreover, both Machiavelli and Nietzsche see it as the "great man's" destiny to legislate values and codes of behavior for the ignorant rabble, and the good-eater once again concurs.[7]

But there's a crucial difference between the "great man" and the good-eater. The "great men" over whom Machiavelli and Nietzsche rhapsodize are majestically contemptuous of humanity. They have no "altruistic" impulse to improve the lot of either individuals or society. They are unabashed buccaneers, not reformers. Their only aim is to use others for their own advancement. As we've already noted, however, the good-eater is a reformer—or at least has managed to persuade himself that he is. Far from seeing himself as a buccaneer, he's convinced that he's a visionary willing to burn himself out in the service of his "noble" plan to reform people. All this of course is egregious self-deception, but it's so thoroughgoing that the good-eater retains to the end the illusion that he acts out of altruism. Even as he lops off heads and poisons enemies in pursuit of the Rational Life, Herod clings to the conviction that everything he does is for the commonweal.

Thirdly, good-eating oughtn't to be confused with old-fashioned hypocrisy. The moral hypocrite is a self-serving dissembler who dons a public persona of rectitude she neither believes nor privately follows. She pretends to be concerned with the well-being of others, but in fact is perfectly willing to use them in order to promote her own interests.

But there's no analogous division between publicly avowed principles and private motives in the good-eater. He really *does* believe that his vision of the good is perfect and that the laws he decrees for others are for their own benefit. How could it be otherwise? As an omnibenevolent God, he has both the know-how and the desire to make people good. Like Herod, he wishes only to make others happy.

Moral Machismo

In *Fear and Trembling*, Søren Kierkegaard asks a question that generations of Jews and Christians have worried over: Why does scripture praise Abraham as a "good" man? Here is a person, Kierkegaard reminds us, who deliberately sets out to slaughter his only son, Isaac. With cold-blooded premeditation he takes the child to a lonely mountaintop, binds his arms, and hoists a dagger to gut him like a sacrificial lamb. The only thing that reprieves Isaac is the angel's last-minute intervention, not any change of heart from Abraham (Gn 22). Surely any reasonable individual must see Abraham's behavior as unconscionably heinous, a horrifying breach of a moral principle accepted by all decent persons: Parents ought not to harm their own children. Yet scripture presents Abraham as an exemplary saint rather than a moral monster. How can this be explained?

The merit of Kierkegaard's analysis is that he refuses to offer a slick, canned response to this conundrum. Instead, he turns the puzzle this way and that, looking at it from a number of different angles, earnestly trying to make sense of it. The conclusion he finally and hesitantly—in "fear and trembling"—offers is that humans owe "an absolute duty toward God," and that when the Infinite commands, obedience takes precedence over fidelity to conventional standards of ethical obligation.

"This is a paradox," comments Kierkegaard, "which does not permit of mediation." Abraham is a true saint, a "knight of faith," because he is willing to suffer the moral condemnation of his fellows for the sake of obeying God's will. Although everything in Abraham recoiled at God's order to sacrifice the dearly beloved Isaac, he "evacuated himself in [service to] the Infinite," recognizing that revelation necessarily supersedes human notions of what's ethical and what's not. Kierkegaard concludes that "the story of Abraham contains therefore a teleological suspension of the ethical" to remind us that God's will rather than our limited understanding of what's "good" or "evil" is the final word in all matters.[8]

Read in this light, the Abraham-Isaac story is a powerful parable about our utter dependence on God. But Kierkegaard's analysis unintentionally sheds light on an essential mechanism of good-eating as well. The good-eater is quite happy to grant that God's will always and everywhere supersedes conventional ethical principles, codes of conduct, and individual opinions. The demonic twist, however, is this: Since the good-eater takes Godhood for himself by claiming it is his legislating will that is the supreme standard of value, he absolves himself of any obligation to abide by the ethical law he universalizes for everybody else. He (and he alone) is not bound by the moral principles he decrees for mere humans, and may actually violate them with impunity for the "greater" *telos* or purpose of bringing about his vision of the perfect society.

Good-eating Herod, for example, imposes on his subjects an ethical program that morally and legally forbids actions such as robbery, killing, and physical violence. He does this for their "own good"; the utopian Rational Life, after all, is not possible if citizens swipe park benches, counterfeit coins, or molest one another. Yet Herod is perfectly willing to "send for the military" in order to force conformity to the moral order he's decreed. He punishes the rabble by seizing their property, intimidates them with fire and sword, and even slays them if he must, all in order to make them good. His assumption of divine moral wisdom, in other words, convinces him that he's above the very principles he insists are absolute for others. For the sake of bringing about the "good," he refuses to be bound by the "ethical." Such is the warped logic of good-eating's reformism.

The good-eater may not be a hypocrite, but the ethical authority he bestows upon himself canonizes a double normative standard that clearly reveals what may be called his "moral machismo." Since his normative wisdom is more acute than everyone else's, his duty—and his right—is to dictate their values and behavior. Since everyone else's normative wisdom is flawed, it is their duty—as well as their privilege—to conform to the good-eater's prescriptions and prohibitions. Out of a sense of divine duty, the good-eater refuses to tie his own hands by conforming to the standards he expects everyone else to live up to. He marches to his own drumbeat, because he and he alone has the absolute foresight to know where the parade is headed. Everyone else, quite properly, follows his lead.

But like all varieties of machismo, the good-eater's version is based on a falsehood. He does not possess divine moral insight, nor is he above "ordinary" norms of decency. Once again, no one is Good but God alone, and the good-eater, for all his frantic efforts to claim divinity for himself, is but a fallible person—a "mediocrity," as Simone Weil put it. His misguided attempt to set up a double normative standard, one for himself and one for everybody else, only underscores his lack of true insight into both his own nature and the nature of divine Goodness.

Godlust

Most of us probably recognize the taint of moral machismo in one or two of our acquaintances. The overpowering mother who with the "best intentions" in the world refuses to cut the apron strings; the boss who drowns his employees in training sessions and interoffice memos to make them "better" workers; the academic mentor who zealously molds students in her own image; the spouse on a mission to "improve" his or her partner: We all know such holier-than-thou-ers, and like the Pharisee in Luke's gospel (18:11) we thank God we're not one of them.

But the plank is in our own eyes; the worm of Godlust twists in our own smug hearts. It takes but a little honest reflection to see that each of us suffers to one extent or another from the moral machismo we so eagerly point out and condemn in others. It's not just wild-eyed reformers with their various "isms" who see themselves as normative authorities; we all tend to assume moral superiority. With almost knee-jerk predictability we bristle at having values "imposed" on us, and we fiercely resist being evaluated in light of someone else's normative standards. "Who are *you* to judge *me*?" we indignantly ask our critics. "I answer to nothing but my own conscience! Keep your morality to yourself!" But when our hackles rise in this way, the underlying (even if unarticulated) message is that *we* are the final arbiters of our own values, that *we* inherently possess the requisite normative wisdom to determine the good for ourselves—that we are, in a word, ethically *causa sui*.

If we stopped here, we would fall into the camp of ethical subjectivism. But typically we don't stop. Loyal to the logic of moral machismo, we sanctimoniously refuse others the ethical self-sufficiency we grant ourselves. Instead, we claim the authority to set other people straight about how they should comport themselves. Our vantage point, we assure them, is objective and unsullied; theirs is not, because they're "too close" to the situation. As a consequence, we know better than they what's genuinely in their best interests, and we conscientiously go about the business of "reforming" them.

Finally, we're skilled at cutting ourselves slack when we perform actions we self-righteously condemn in others. We argue that there are "extenuating circumstances" that absolve us from culpability—"don't judge me until you've walked in my shoes!"—or, like Herod, we justify our violations of conventional norms by claiming that our actions are for a "higher good." At the same time, however, we're loath to admit similar extenuating circumstances when it comes to the behavior of others, or to allow them the privilege of disregarding norms for the sake of higher goods. We permit ourselves a teleological suspension of the ethical that we disdain to give to others. But as good-eaters, we don't do so cynically or self-servingly; our motives are "pure." Our only concern is the moral improvement of both individuals and society. We want people good and social relations just, and we know how to achieve both these goals. All that others need do is give us free rein—which means, of course, that they submit to our superior vision of the good. Moral machismo's double standard crops up again: Do what I say, not what I do.[9]

Raising Kane

So far we've seen *what* the good-eater does when he arrogantly declares his will the supreme moral standard. But the question of precisely *how* he goes wrong is still unresolved. Just what is the blind spot that so clouds his vision of the true nature of the Good?

We can begin to answer this question by taking a look at what's likely the greatest American film ever made: Orson

Welles's 1941 *Citizen Kane*. The movie's eponymous hero, Charles Foster Kane, is a twentieth-century archetype of good-eating. In exploring Kane's rise and fall, Welles brilliantly uncovers for us the heart of the good-eater's spiritual brokenness.[10]

Kane is a Godluster who, with predictable rapacity, is out to devour the planet. As one of the world's wealthiest men, he's in a good position to do so. Initially he seeks to slake his hunger by collecting things: cash, gems, businesses, railroads, apartment buildings, entire city blocks. But these hors d'oeuvres only whet the appetite and make Kane ravenous for the more solid fare of Godhood. So he proceeds to load up his plate with Truth, Beauty, and the Good.

Kane gobbles up Truth by purchasing a nearly bankrupt newspaper and sinking millions of dollars into it in order to make it the nation's most widely circulated daily. But as an editor and publisher, he isn't interested in just reporting the news. Instead, he creates it by using the printed word to manipulate and even fabricate events. "If the headline is big enough," he tells his staff, "it makes the news big enough." And Kane is a genius at writing headlines. He uses them to sway public opinion, influence political decisions, and even create international crises. He's the original spin doctor. His interpretations and angles *become* truth. As Kane explains, "People will think what I tell them to think."[11]

Kane gobbles up Beauty in two ways. First, he holds controlling interests in a multitude of industries—timber, mining, shipping—which generate their colossal profits by raping the natural order. Thus the entire planet becomes Kane's to exploit and control. Even animals are no exception: By the end of his life, Kane has a private zoo that outstrips any public one in the world. Second, Kane makes beauty his own by feverishly buying up as many objets d'art as he can amass. His fantastically lavish estate, Xanadu, is glutted with statues, paintings, jewelry, and even entire castle walls and cathedral facades marauded from every country on earth. Kane doesn't horde these objects because he appreciates their beauty; for every treasure on display, there's a score of others in storage he's never bothered to uncrate. His only motive is possession: to devour and make his own all the beauty in the world.

But alas: The God-who-devour's palate is easily jaded. After a few years of truth- and beauty-eating, Kane finds himself increasingly dissatisfied, and slides into Godlust's culminating stage by directing his appetite to the Good. He's already sovereign lord over truth and nature. The only thing left to conquer is people. So Kane proceeds to add omnibenevolence to his already crowded resumé by eating the Good. He decides to devote himself to social and political "reform."

Actually, Kane has always nibbled at the Good. As we've seen, human-Gods never consider themselves bound by the feeble norms of society and tradition. They're above the ethical, independent of conventional morality. They make their own rules and walk their own paths. "There's only one person in the world to decide what I'm going to do," Kane declares early on in his career, "and that's me!" But Kane graduates from nibbling to full-scale gobbling when he decides he's the one man able to redress all of society's ills (which of course means he's not a "man" at all, but a God). Harnessing the power of his personal fortune and newspaper empire, he "altruistically" prepares to establish God's kingdom on earth by running for public office. His political campaign revolves around two points: a relentless denunciation of his incumbent opponent's corruption and a messianic promise to sacrifice himself in service to the "working man, slum child, the underpaid, the underprivileged, the underfed."

At a glance, Kane seems genuinely idealistic. The political corruption and social oppression his campaign targets are real enough; so are his reformist aspirations. He's honest when he says he wants to help the underdog, and there's no reason to doubt that he would work to realize his vision of the good life with all the dedicated energy of Auden's Herod. But when one looks a bit more carefully, Kane's zealous idealism reveals itself as vintage moral machismo. He condemns moral and political corruption in others, but excuses identical behavior in himself by arguing that deception and manipulation are necessary means to securing election and doing good. Thus the great God Kane suspends the ethical when it comes to his own conduct, thereby canonizing the double standard characteristic of good-eating. Moreover, Kane's arrogant promise that he and he alone can offer salvation to society's oppressed comes with a high price tag: absolute submission to his moral will, his imperious vision of what's good for them, his determination of what's in everyone's best interests. Kane as God/Goodness is the almighty source of moral truth, and his reformation of society will consist in remaking humans into what he thinks they should be. He commands; others obey. This is the proper relationship between an all-good Messiah and fallible mortals.

In one of the film's most revelatory scenes, the depth of Kane's good-eating is plumbed by Jedidiah Leland, a genuine idealist horrified and repulsed by Kane's increasingly obvious Godlust. It's in Leland's indictment of Kane that we find a hint of good-eating's fundamental failure:

> You talk about the people as though you own them, as
> though they belong to you. For as long as I can remember
> you've talked about giving the people their "rights," as if
> you could make them a present of liberty as a reward for
> services rendered....
>
> You don't care about anything except yourself! You just
> wanna persuade people that you love them so much that
> they oughta love you back. Only you want love on you
> own terms—something to be played *your* way according
> to *your* rules!

Kane, unfazed by Leland's denunciation, smilingly quips:
"A toast, Jedediah, to love on my own terms. Those are the
only terms anybody ever knows." Kane can afford to be flip.
Why should a God heed the churlish whinings of a mortal?
Even after the voters spectacularly reject him and destroy
once and for all his prospects of a political career, Kane
refuses to acknowledge that there was anything perverse
about his self-appointment as their Messiah. A God cannot
be mistaken. So with olympian resignation he sighs that
"it's their loss" and retreats to Xanadu, the cavernous,
echo-ridden temple the great God Kane has erected to himself. He lives out the remainder of his days there, convinced
to the very end that the world threw away its one chance of
salvation when it rejected his moral lordship.

Jedidiah Leland put his finger on the pulse of good-eating
when he accused Kane of demanding love on his own terms, as
well as when he opined later in the film that Kane "just didn't
have any [love] to give" to others. The fundamental way good-
eaters go wrong is in failing—or, more accurately, refusing—to
see that the essence of divine Goodness, and consequently of
any and all human attempts to be and do good, is *love*. Fixated
as Kane and other good-eaters are on their egoistic drive to

raise themselves to the level of God so that they can manipulate and control persons, they are as incapable of genuine love *for* others as they are of accepting genuine love *from* them. As Leland said and Kane conceded, the good-eater *gives* "love" on his own terms—absolute sovereignty—and *accepts* it on his own terms—total obedience. But this of course is not love at all. The double standard canonized by the good-eater's moral machismo; the privilege he reserves for himself of suspending the norms he universalizes for everyone else; the self-bestowed mandate to force others to obey and to punish them ruthlessly if they resist his moral legislation; the demand for lockstep conformity to his absolute vision of the Good: These, and not love, are the marks of the demonic, of the God-who-devours, of a Moloch who takes but does not give.

Put another way, good-eaters such as Herod and Kane emphasize *law* at the expense of *love*, and thereby preach what Thomas Merton so aptly calls the "moral theology of the devil." "Not love but punishment is the fulfillment of the Law. The Law must devour everything, even God"[12]—which means that the Lawgiver becomes God. Universalized by the good-eater's supreme moral authority and enforced by his iron will, Law, unsullied by weaknesses such as compassion or empathy, becomes the final measure of value. The Law—or what Auden's Herod calls "Justice"—is antiseptically impartial, regarding all (except of course the supreme legislator) equally. Individual personalities mean nothing to the Law; in its eyes, persons aren't concrete entities with unique hopes, fears, strengths and weaknesses so much as abstractions all cut from the same social cloth. Their only function is to obey the Law, which of course means to obey the will of the good-eating lawmaker. Jedidiah Leland was correct: The good-eater acts as if he owns people, and he shuffles them about with the calculative coldness of a chess master. Chess pieces are made to be manipulated, not loved.

It only makes sense that the good-eater focuses on Law rather than love. Genuine love, as we'll see shortly, is a self-emptying that joyfully works for the welfare of the beloved. It gives itself unconditionally, expecting nothing in return. But the Law is merely an extension of the good-eater's ego. Supreme legislators such as Herod and Kane claim that they universalize their visions of the good in order to help others, but this is subterfuge. Their primary motive is to divinize themselves by transforming their wills into Law. Thus the good-eater, far from emptying himself in the service of others, actually reverses the process. He demands that others empty themselves in service to his will. The God-who-devours cannot love. Like the law-crunching Pharisee of Jesus' time, he does not have God's Love within him (Jn 5:42). So he can only consume. The closest the God-who-devours comes to an expression of love is nodding with paternalistic approval at his subjects when they line up to be eaten—for their "own good."

This is the fatal blind spot of the good-eater. This is how he goes wrong. There is no Good without love. In refusing to love others or to allow them opportunities to love, the good-eater does not, cannot, work in their (or his) best interests. But he has no choice except to substitute his lawlike will for love, because to admit that love is the Good is to acknowledge his own lack of divinity, and this above all else he fears to do. When we love, we experience God-in-us. When we open ourselves to love from others, we experience God-in-them. We recognize, in short, that love points beyond the self and its frenzy to legislate toward a supremely loving Source whose energy, as Jonathan Edwards said, harmonizes all creation, and who is the ultimate Good precisely because it is ultimate Love.

Good-eaters, if they remain loyal to the logic of their God-lust, have no choice but to cut themselves off—and even worse, try to cut others off as well—from the Love that challenges their sovereignty. Thus their drive to replace it with the reign of Law. But when they do so, they exile themselves—and attempt to exile us—to the desolate loneliness of a fortress mountain or the mocking emptiness of a Xanadu. There's a hefty price to be paid for raising Kane: a fall from deep to deeper into a loveless and hence Godless abyss. As Dostoevsky and Georges Bernanos after him said, Hell is not to love.[13] Centuries earlier, the beloved disciple John put it even more bleakly: "He who does not love abides in death" (1 Jn 3:14).

Three Faces of Divine Love

Only God is Good, because love is good and only God is pure Love. But how can we understand what it means to say that God is Love/Goodness? We may turn to scripture for an answer to this question.

The Bible is an unveiling of God's face that provides us with a cumulative and complex portrait of the Divine. It is cumulative because it traces over a period of several thousand years humanity's progressive understanding of God's alethic unconcealment. It is complex because the Being who unveils for us displays inexhaustible depth and meaning. But there is a single shining-forth that threads together the cumulative revealings: God is Love. God acts righteously and justly, but these qualities are always grounded in divine *chesed* or "steadfast loving-kindness" and *agape* or "self-emptying beneficence." Love is ever the primary Good.

Because divine Love is limitless and unqualified, it is ultimately incomprehensible. Even in its most concrete revelation,

Jesus the Christ, the depth of God's Love remains mysterious; as we saw in chapter 2, every alethic unconcealing of divine Being carries at its heart a concealing. Scripture recognizes the impossibility of a full conceptual grasp of divine Love, and so tries to say something about it by way of analogy and metaphor. We may not be able to describe precisely what God as Love *is*, but we can say what God as Love is *like*.

In attempting to convey the essence of divine *chesed* and *agape*, the scriptures most frequently appeal to three concrete similes. One is of God as Parent: Divine Love is like the original love of a mother or father for a child. Another is of God as Spouse or Lover: God's Love for us is similar to the joyful and passionate exuberance of romantic love. Finally, God is often referred to as the Shepherd: God's love for humans is like the beneficent care of a herder for his or her flock. Thus the Old and New Testaments provide us with three faces or aspects of one and the same loving God. Taken together, they do not exhaust the meaning of divine Love. But they do point us in the right direction.

God as Parent. The most ancient way in which the Bible expresses God's Love is by speaking of God as a parent who brings forth, loves, and nurtures children. Even though the parenthood of God is implied in the creation account—"So God created man in his own image...; male and female he created them" (Ex1:27)—the first explicit Old Testament reference is found in Exodus (4:22) when God refers to Israel as "my firstborn son." Deuteronomy (32:6) calls God a "father" who created, established, and guides his children; Isaiah (64:8) echoes the sentiment when he proclaims: "O Lord, thou art our Father; we are the clay, and thou art our potter." Jeremiah suggests the parent-child intimacy of the relationship between God and humans by referring to the Divine as "my Father" (3:4,19), while Hosea states it in a more direct and touching way: "When Israel was a child, I [God] loved him, and out of Egypt I called my son" (11:1). Psalm 103 also assures us that God loves humans with tender, fatherly compassion.

The Old Testament intuition that God is like a loving parent reaches new heights in the New Testament's good news of the incarnation. God now is not only the Parent of humankind but also the Father of the Messiah, and the intimacy between God and Jesus, who endearingly refers to God as "Abba" (Mk 14:36), serves as an exemplar of the intimacy between God and humans. Jesus also refers to God as "Father" in the prayer of adoration and petition he taught his disciples (Lk 11:2). Later, Paul follows Jesus' lead by likewise calling God "Abba" (Rom 8:15; Gal 4:6), and in his Letter to the Ephesians (3:14–15) invokes God's benevolent Parenthood as the model for mortal parents. In his first epistle, John expresses the intimacy between the divine Parent and mortals in an especially tender way: "See what love the Father has given us, that we should be called children of God; and so we are....Beloved, we are God's children now" (1 Jn 3:1–2).

The scriptural likening of divine Love to parental love suggests a number of meanings, but the two most salient ones are that God's Love is *original* and *unconditionally sustaining*. The very act of parental procreation is one of love, a generative outflowing of the mother's and father's vitality. The child is loved long before it's ever capable of reciprocating love; it is loved while yet in the womb, and that love continues while the child is still an unaware infant. The child is conceived and nurtured, in other words, in a milieu of love, and when it eventually begins to love the parents it does so in response to their original love for it. Similarly, God's creation of the world and its human inhabitants is an outpouring of divine Love that serves as the foundation for our subsequent love of God and one another. We experience God's Love before we experience anything else. Our embryonic hearts respond to its call, pulsate with its energy. "We love," says John, "because God first loved us" (1 Jn 4:19).

Because parental love is original or prior to the child's actual birth, it is also unconditional. The child has done nothing to "deserve" its parents' love, nor need it. It is loved absolutely, without reservation, simply because it is. Moreover, the unconditionality of this love sustains the child throughout its various stages of life. Since parental love is not based on desert, a mother and father's love for the child endures absolutely regardless of whether the child accepts or rejects that love in later life, and regardless of whether the child grows into saint or sinner. The safety net of parental love endures; the loving milieu into which the child was born abides.

Certainly scripture's richest expression of God the Parent's unconditionally sustaining Love is Jesus' parable about the prodigal son (Lk 15:11–32). The father's love endures even when the son, in a gross act of filial disrespect, demands his share of the inheritance and leaves home to pursue a wastrel's life. Despite his self-centered dissipation, the prodigal son always carries with him a flickering remembrance of the unconditionality of his father's sustaining love. When he finds himself penniless and starving, he senses that his father will not scorn his plea for aid. But the unlimited extent of the parent's love is not fully appreciated until the prodigal son returns to find that his father welcomes him with open arms and tears of rejoicing. So it is with God the Father/Mother, whose arms are always open to welcome us back home with love and joy. Once established by God's original generative act of love, the bond between mortals and God is never sundered by the divine Parent. It endures forever, despite our best efforts to rupture it.[14]

God as Spouse. The loving father celebrated the prodigal son's homecoming with joyful music and dancing. This suggests another aspect of God's love for humans: its sheer *exuberance*. Divine love is neither dour nor gloomily serious. It sparkles with the gaiety, excitement, enthusiasm, and total engagement of romantic ardor. God's love for us is like the love of a husband burning for his wife or a wife burning for her husband. God is not only our Parent. God is also the Lover who passionately yearns for an intimacy that trills with "the voice of mirth and the voice of gladness, the voice of the bridegroom and the voice of the bride" (Jer 16:9).

This image of God as Lover or Spouse lies at the heart of two Old Testament books: Hosea and the Song of Songs. Hosea famously likens God to a cuckolded spouse who nonetheless is both willing and eager to reconcile with his faithless partner, humanity. As one would expect, emotions run high in this tale of betrayed intimacy: The pain and despair of the forsaken Spouse's pleas for reconciliation at times are almost too much for the reader to bear. But even in the midst of such heartbreak the crackle of divine Love's passion for the faithless partner comes through. Speaking to "adulterous" humanity, God longs for the day when "you [again] will call me, 'My husband'" (2:16). In pursuit of such a rapprochement, the Lord resolves to once more woo Israel with all the ardor of the original courtship:

> I will allure her,
> and bring her into the wilderness,
> and speak tenderly to her.
> And there I will give her vineyards,
> and make the Valley of Achor a door of hope.

And there she shall answer as in the days of her youth,
    as at the time when she came out of the Land of Egypt.
      (2:14–15)

On the joyful day when Israel returns to her senses and realizes that God is her one true Lover, the Lord hopefully and joyfully promises "I will betroth you to me for ever" (2:19).

Hosea conveys the depth of God the Spouse's passion for humanity through a tale of unrequited love. But the Old Testament's Song of Songs is a more happy love story that celebrates the erotic passion and ardor of the Bridegroom for the bride and the bride for the Bridegroom. God is "like a gazelle or a young stag upon the mountains of spices" (8:14) ablaze with longing for his "sister," his "bride." He stands in the beloved's garden and woos her with night-songs of adoration:

Behold, you are beautiful, my love,
behold, you are beautiful!
Your eyes are doves
    behind your veil....
Your lips are like a scarlet thread,
    and your mouth is lovely.
Your cheeks are like halves of a pomegranate
    behind your veil....
Your two breasts are like two fawns,
    twins of a gazelle,
    that feed among the lilies....
You are all fair, my love;
    there is no flaw in you....
You have ravished my heart, my sister, my bride,
    you have ravished my heart with a glance of your eyes.
(4:1,3,5,7,9)

The ardor of the divine Lover is fully reciprocated by the human bride. "O that you would kiss me with the kisses of your mouth!" she exclaims, "For your love is better than wine!" (1:1). The blandishments of her gazelle-like Lover have awakened her heart (5:2) and, "sick with love" (5:8), she longs to fly to his arms. "Make haste, my beloved!" she calls (8:14). Nothing can keep the two apart, nor can any misfortune lessen their ardor for one another. "For love is strong as death," and

> Its flashes are flashes of fire,
>   a most vehement flame.
> Many waters cannot quench love,
>   neither can floods drown it. (8:6–7)[15]

The same sense of divine Love as a joyfully passionate eros is expressed in the New Testament's frequent references to the relationship between God and humans in terms of marriage. In the ancient Near East, a wedding was a time of joyful celebration, usually lasting at least a week, in which friends and relatives of the betrothed couple gathered to celebrate nuptial love. The kingdom of God which Jesus declares already among us is likened to a wedding feast, and Jesus himself is the Bridegroom (Mt 22:1–14; 25:1–12). All are invited to the marriage festivities, even though, sadly, many will refuse to attend (Mt 22:1–14).

The arrival of Christ the ardently passionate Bridegroom is an occasion for great rejoicing. In reply to pharisaic criticisms of his disciples' gay lightheartedness, Jesus asks "Can the wedding guests mourn as long as the bridegroom is with them?" (Mt 9:15). It's significant that Jesus' first public miracle, the turning of water into wine, occurs at a wedding feast (Jn 2:1–11). God's love is exuberant, and it wishes everyone to share in the exuberance; there's always enough and more of divine Love to go around. Finally, John's Revelation is sprinkled with references that liken God's love to the joyful ardor of courtship and marriage. All humans are invited to "the marriage of the Lamb" (19:7), and thereby "blessed" (19:9)—not as guests, but as those betrothed to the divine Bridegroom (21:9; 22:17). At the end of time, the new Jerusalem, the heavenly city, will be as radiantly "prepared as a bride adorned for her husband" (21:2).

The comparison of divine Love to nuptial love in both the Old and New Testaments underscores the fact that God's love is an occasion for the great joy and intense passion characteristic of romantic exhilaration. It is a love so complete that it invigorates our bodies as well as our hearts and souls. When it flows down to us—and it is everflowing—it elicits laughter and singing and dancing. God's love for us is also sharply all-consuming in the way that romantic love always is, and in turn elicits a total reponse from us. The Bride longs for her Lover, her Bridegroom, to bound down from the spicey mountains with graceful gazelle strides and sweep her off her feet. When he comes, how can she not be jubilant?

God as Shepherd. If the oldest scriptural expression of God's Love is couched in terms of parental love, and the most endearing one is a lyrical appeal to spousal or romantic love, certainly the image most frequently invoked by Old and New Testament authors alike is divine Love as the *solicitous guidance* of a shepherd. God is the overseer, we the flock, and the divine overseer protects and leads us with unfailing and self-sacrificing devotion.

The role of a shepherd is neither as revered as that of a parent nor exciting as that of a lover. But it is an absolutely essential one. Sheep need constant and vigilant guidance; otherwise, the defenseless creatures are easily led astray and lost. They must be protected from predatory beasts who would slay and devour them (Is 31:4; Ez 35:5; Am 3:12; Jn 10:12) or thieves who lay in wait to carry them off (Gn 31:39; Jn 10:1,8,10). In the hands of a good overseer, the sheep thrive. In the hands of a bad one, they perish (Is 40:11; 49:9–10; Mi 4:6–8; 7:14).

The Old Testament, particularly in the psalms, contains numerous references to God as the supreme Shepherd (Psalm 23 is the best-known example, but see also 28:9; 74:1; 77:20; 78:52–53; 80:1; 95:7; 100:3; 121:3–8). By far the lengthiest and most detailed treatment of God as Shepherd appears in Ezekiel, where the prophet devotes an entire chapter (34) to the comparison.

In Ezekiel, the unconcealment of divine Love as Shepherd-Love is occasioned by God's wrath against the false priestly shepherds of the day who have "scattered" rather than guided their human flock. "Ho, shepherds of Israel who have been feeding yourselves!" thunders God,

> Should not shepherds feed the sheep? You eat the fat, you clothe yourselves with the wool, you slaughter the fatlings; but you do not feed the sheep. The weak you have not strengthened, the sick you have not healed, the crippled you have not bound up, the strayed you have not brought back, the lost you have not sought, and with force and harshness you have ruled them. (34:2–4)

Therefore, declares God, "Behold, I, I myself will search for my sheep, and will seek them out" (34:11). "I will seek the lost, and I will bring back the strayed, and I will bind up the crippled, and I will strengthen the weak, and the fat and the strong I will watch over. I will feed them in justice [and] they shall no more be consumed with hunger" (34:16, 29).

The constancy and compassion with which Ezekiel's divine Shepherd lovingly watches over humans is raised to an even more profound level in the New Testament's understanding of Jesus the Christ. Jesus is "the great shepherd of the sheep" (Heb 13:20), the "Shepherd and Guardian of souls" (1 Pt 2:25), the "chief Shepherd" (1 Pt 5:4) who cares for his "little flock" (Lk 12:32). As such, he has compassion on those humans who seek direction (Mt 9:36; Mk 6:34), and is especially solicitous of those who have "gone astray" (Mt 10:6; 15:24; 18:12; Lk 15:3–7; Jn 10:3-5). But now two additional aspects of divine shepherding are revealed. The first is that God's Shepherd-Love of humans is great enough to burn itself out in their service. God does not merely watch over and guide mortals, but willingly sacrifices himself for their well-being. As Jesus says of himself, "I am the good shepherd. The good shepherd lays down his life for the sheep" (Jn 10:11). The second new revelation of God's Shepherd-Love is that it is all-inclusive. Divine love is not selective or discriminatory, but instead is bestowed without partiality upon all men and women. "I have other sheep that are not of this fold," says Jesus. "I must bring them also, and they will heed my voice. So there shall be one flock, one shepherd" (Jn 10:16).

Human Loving

We've seen that a corollary of scripture's likening of divine Love to parental and spousal love is that humans should seek to emulate it in their own lives. Paul says that the Love of God as Parent should serve as the model for mortal parents, and the Song of Songs reminds us that we ought to burn with something of the infinite passion the divine Lover feels for us. The same scriptural lesson also holds for God's Shepherd-Love. Just as God compassionately guides and protects us, even to the point of self-sacrifice, so men and women who become spiritual leaders (and all of us are called to such leadership) ought to do likewise. Jesus, for example, tells Peter to "tend my sheep" and "feed my sheep" in loving service (Jn 21:15–17). In a similar vein, Paul reminds the Ephesian elders of their duty to care for their "flock," the "church of God" (Acts 20: 28–30), and in his epistle to them (Eph 4:11) explicitly calls them *poimenas* or shepherds (usually translated as "pastors").

In short, humans are called by scripture to imitate and reciprocate divine Love right down the line. Just as God is a Parent, a Spouse, and a Shepherd, so must we be. Just as God's Goodness is Love, so we emulate and participate in the Good when we love.

The good man or woman is not an iron-willed, value-decreeing Herod or Kane who "altruistically" but lovelessly whips people into shape. The good person is one who loves God and his or her fellows with the unconditionality of a parent, the joy of a spouse, and the compassionate responsibility of a shepherd. The good person loves even when his or her love is ignored or spurned, patiently and hopefully enduring the pain of rejection for the sake of the beloved. The good person gives himself or herself to the beloved, seeking nothing in return. The good person guides as a shepherd does, even to the point of laying down his or her own life, but carefully refrains from pushing loved ones beyond their endurance or hastily driving them where they're not ready to go. The good person longs to kiss and be kissed, knowing that "many waters cannot quench love, neither can floods drown it." The good person, in a word, wants love on God's terms, not on his or hers.

How can we break our addiction to good-eating, relinquishing the sinful urge to set up our own wills as the sole determiners of the Good? How can we surrender ourselves to the God who is Love and in the process more fully reflect that Love? How can we so imitate God's Goodness that we become parents, lovers, and shepherds in our own right?

The first thing to keep in mind is that we are made in God's image, shot through and through with incandescent sparks of divine Being. Regardless of how self-destructively we hurtle ourselves into the darkness of the abyss, we remain, by virtue of our deiform natures, unbreakably connected to the God who is Love. By God's grace, then, we always carry within us the spiritual propensity to love, even if it's buried deeply beneath the grime of Godlust. Because the healing waters of divine Love percolate within us, we are capable of living up to the great commandment to love God and our fellows with all our hearts, souls, and minds (Mt 22:37–40). God does not ask more of us than we are capable of giving, nor does God ask anything of us he does not also freely give. Just as God loves, so are we called to love. "A new commandment I give to you, that you love one another; even as I have loved you, that you also love one another" (Jn 13:34).

What this means is that *we* are the worldly signals of transcendence that point to divine Goodness/Love. Worldly truth gestures at the *aletheia* that reveals God's Being, and natural beauty points to the Beauty of God's Holiness; but humanity itself is the earthly reflection of divine Love. God's Love shines through each and every one of us; God's Goodness radiates from our acts of love for one another. Our duty and privilege as Christians is to attune our wills to God's so that the divine Love/Goodness already within us comes to the surface and blossoms, making us one with the supreme Parent,

Lover, Shepherd. The kingdom of God's Love, the reign of divine Goodness, is here and now, within our hearts. We are called to rediscover it, to embrace it, and to enable our sisters and brothers to embrace it as well, so that all of us may progress toward the deification that is our common destiny.

More specifically, living the parental, spousal, and shepherd Love that God is means that we who are made in the image of divine Love cultivate rather than flee from *precarious poverty*; that we sensitize ourselves to God's *presence* in everyone we meet; that we sow love with unabashed *profligacy*; and that we help others to learn the ways of love by exercising *passionate restraint*.

Precarious Poverty. Good-eating, like all manifestations of Godlust, is an attempt to imperialize egoistic will, to posit the self as the center of gravity around which creation revolves. Such is the antidote the Godluster hopes will palliate his oppressive sense of ontological anxiety. But as we've seen, this hope is illusory. The self is too mediocre to live up to the divine status it craves, and its aching awareness of its own inadequacy is exacerbated rather than alleviated when it absents God and thereby exiles itself from God.

If the good-eater is ever to escape the forlornly loveless Xanadu to which his boundless arrogance banishes him, he must wean himself—cultivate Ignatius's *indiferençia*—from his self-destructive allegiance to the imperial demands of self. Good is not an aggrandizement of ego that grants the self the right to ordain laws for others from which it is "teleologically" exempt; instead, good is an annihilation of ego that recognizes the self's fragility and fundamental dependence upon the supreme Source of Love. But the good-eater who takes his own will as the final determination of value is unable to see this.

Obsessively convinced that he's the saving God, he fears and avoids any challenge to his sovereignty. Egoistically concentrated as he is on "improving" others, he clings to the deluded machismo of moral superiority.

A first step, then, in recollecting our innate connection with the Source of Goodness and Love and thereby returning to the path of love is to embrace spiritual precarity and poverty. We can only begin to love when we voluntarily step out of the self, put off the old Adam, and forsake the selfish "I" for "they." We've seen that scripture expresses love through the metaphors of parenting, spousing, and shepherding, and each of these represents an emptying of the self in service to the beloved. Only an individual who no longer fixates on the self, who is liberated from the lust for moral authority and moral privilege, can make room for others. Only an individual who realizes that he doesn't hold all the cards in the game of life can reach out in empathy and compassion to the other players. Only an individual who forgets himself can love.

This is the secret behind Jesus' promise that the "poor in spirit" are genuinely blessed (Mt 5:3). They have stripped themselves of the moral machismo that holds the good-eater back from truly loving and serving others. They have relinquished the good-eater's conceit of invulnerability so that they can genuinely make themselves available to others—and, just as important, to allow others to be available to them. The poor in spirit embrace poverty by giving up the riches that the good-eater holds dear. They voluntarily surrender a life of power and control for one of continuous precarity—the risk of giving and inviting love, of helping others and confessing their own need for help in return. In doing so they are blessed because they imitate the self-giving characteristic of divine Love. They discover that the ego denial so repugnant to the Godluster in fact is a passport into the life abundant. The paradox of precarious poverty is that, once embraced, it fulfills precisely because it empties. In dying to self, we make room for God and our fellow humans.

Presence. The good-eater relates to abstractions rather than people. Seated high on his throne, he's so distant from those to whom he "altruistically" hands down moral laws that he never gets to know them as concrete individuals. They remain faceless statistics in one of Herod's government reports or anonymous members of the "underprivileged, underpaid, underfed" set Charles Foster Kane makes speeches about.

But genuine love sees the person; love relates to the woman or man rather than to a bloodless abstraction; love focuses on the individual, not the concept. At the end of the day, what counts isn't theoretical assent to an ideal such as the Rational Life, but a lived assent and wholehearted commitment to persons. And a necessary condition for this kind of love is the awareness that there's something preeminently lovable in each and every human we encounter.

That good and great twentieth-century lover Dorothy Day tells a story about the time she despairingly asked a priest "how God could love a man who came home and beat up his wife and children in a drunken rage." She says that the priest shook his head sadly and simply replied: "God loves only Jesus, God sees only Jesus."[16] There is a great truth in the priest's words. When God gazes upon fallible, fragile human beings, the God who is Parent-Love looks beyond the children's prodigality to embrace only the lovable in them. Splintered and bespattered though they may be, God sees only the good in them. If we would imitate divine Love, we too must sensitize ourselves to the lovableness that radiates from all humans—not just the ones we approve of, the ones we respect, but all: the weakest, the most broken, the most derelict. As Dorothy's priest intimated, their lovableness is the presence of Christ within them. When we encounter others, especially those who are wounded, we encounter the mystery of Christ, and what we do to and for them we do to and for Christ (Mt 25:40). As Dorothy herself subsequently came to realize,

> This blindness of love, this folly of love—this seeing Christ in others, everywhere, and not seeing the ugly, the obvious, the dirty, the sinful—this means we do not see the faults of others—only our own. We see only Christ in them. We have eyes only for our beloved, ears for his voice.[17]

When the good-eater looks at people, he sees chess pieces. But when the lover who has impoverished herself by forsaking ego looks at another person, she sees someone made in God's image and imbued with the loving and good spirit of Christ. She is "intensely aware," as Dorothy says, of that person's Christ-reflected "beauty, virtues, strengths," and accordingly wishes to serve and celebrate rather than command and manipulate.[18]

It mustn't be supposed that the presence of God which shines forth from persons neutralizes or negates their concrete uniqueness or identity for us. Instead, attuning to Christ's powerful presence in others helps us to appreciate more fully their individual gifts and needs. Our identity as concrete personalities is brought to completion by God's presence in our lives. Whenever the lover intuits that divine presence, the transfigurative revelation that originally occurred on Mount Tabor happens again. In seeing people for what they really are, we necessarily see God, and we long to serve both with the fervor of a parent who sacrifices herself for her child. The two great commandments are inseparable: To love persons is to love God, and to love God is to love persons, because we are in Christ and Christ is in us. Love, as Jonathan Edwards saw, is the great harmonizer.

Profligacy. When our embrace of precarious poverty allows us to shed the egoism that blinds us to the presence of Christ's Love and Goodness in all persons, we begin to love. But genuine love is limitless. The Lover longs to lay the world at the beloved's feet, and the unbridled giddiness of his adoration overflows to encompass whomever he meets. The Bride yearns to give herself wholeheartedly to the Bridegroom, and in her joyful exhilaration dances with one and all at the wedding feast. When we love, we do not worry about our just desert or propriety or dividends. We throw caution to the wind and love generously, spontaneously, unstintingly. Human love is and ought to be profligate, because God loves profligately.

One of Jesus' best-loved stories, the parable of the sower (Mt 13:1–24), speaks to the generosity of divine Love. The most obvious point to the parable, as Jesus himself says, is that God's word can take root and bear fruit only if the soul is receptive to it. Some souls are hard and barren, others choked with weeds, and still others have such a thin layer of topsoil that seeds sprout only to wither. But some souls are rich and hungry for the word, and when God sows himself in this kind of soil, wonderful gardens spring up overnight.

There is, however, another lesson that comes across in the parable, and it has to do with the literal act of sowing seed. When we modern-day suburban gardeners do our spring planting, we are sparing in our use of seeds. We dig our neat furrows, carefully measure their lengths in order to calculate how many seeds we ought to use, and then meticulously drop in one seed at a time. This is the way we sow. But in the ancient Near East, spring planting typically involved a wholesale scattering of wheat and barley grains. Seed wasn't scrupulously counted and begrudgingly dropped; it was broadcast in great arching sweeps of the arm and hand without miserly concern for where it fell. As the parable of the sower suggests, the experienced farmer knew that inevitably some of the grain would land on inhospitably barren soil. But he also knew that the more he scattered, the greater were his chances of reaping a rich harvest.

So it is with love. We are called to sow it profligately, not worrying about where it falls or scrambling to calculate cost-benefit ratios. God did not balk at the profligacy of the incarnation; considerations of the cost of total Love simply did not apply. Neither should we hold ourselves back out of anxiety for our well-being. As the disciple John tells us, love casts out fear (1 Jn 4:18). What John implies but doesn't actually say is that the converse equally holds: Fear casts out love. If our anxiety about unforeseen consequences prompts us to dole ourselves out to others in measured droplets, we do not love. Genuine love does not dribble. It freely, extravagantly, ardently, flows, even though such generosity is risky. As Henri Nouwen wrote toward the end of his life: "Jesus says not 'I will take your burden away' but 'Take on God's burden.'"[19]

The profligacy of genuine love can be understood in three ways. In the first place, it's an unlimited and unconditional giving on our parts to the beloved. Like parents, we hold nothing back and expect nothing in return. In loving, we spend our time, our talents, and our energies with such extravagant abandonment that we are impoverished. But this kind of impecunity, as we've seen, leads to spiritual enrichment; a profligate sowing leads to a bountiful harvest (2 Cor 9:6).

In the second place, the profligacy of love is revealed by the fact that it adores the beloved in a complete and unqualified way. This follows from the lover's realization that the face of the other is also the face of the Beloved, the Bridegroom: Christ. When we gaze upon the other with genuine love, we see only the supreme lovability of God shining forth, and we celebrate and serve this presence without reservation. C. S. Lewis once said that there are no "mere" mortals; each human being we meet radiates the divine presence, and thus ought to elicit extravagant and unconditional love from us.[20]

Finally, the profligacy of the lover, like the profligacy of the sower, extends everywhere. Love is not reserved merely for our family members, our friends, our immediate acquaintances. If Christ is present in all people, all people are the proper objects of our love. We've already noted that the love of God the Shepherd is omni-inclusive; *all* people are chosen. If we would imitate the profligacy of supreme Love, we must likewise reach out in love to embrace past, present, and future generations. Everyone who has lived wore Christ's face, everyone who now lives wears Christ's face, and everyone to come will wear Christ's face. When we sow genuine love, our arms swing wide enough to embrace them all.

Passionate Restraint. The profligacy of love to which we are called is ardent, but it doesn't bully. To love is to desire passionately the well-being and flourishing—the good—of the beloved. But such a good cannot be forced on her; this is the way of Law, not love. She cannot be made to be good/loving or coerced into making contact with the Christ within her and within others. So genuine love, boundless though its passion is, voluntarily restrains itself from forcing others in directions they are unwilling or as yet unable to take. Like the nurturance of God the Parent or the solicitude of God the Shepherd, human love patiently beckons to the beloved, tenderly shows the way, gently guides. But it does not smother or drive. Love is an invitation and a gift, not a cattle prod, an enabling (*aition*), not a making. It is passionate restraint.

One of the richest reflections on the passionate restraint characteristic of genuine love comes to us from the theologian and novelist Frederick Buechner. In his third volume of memoirs, Buechner recounts the painful time in his life when one of his daughters "began to stop eating." Buechner tried everything he could to help his daughter overcome her anorexia. But "no rational argument, no dire medical warning, no pleading or cajolery or bribery would make this young woman [I] loved eat normally again." On the contrary, all his "meddling" attempts to rescue her seemed only to strengthen her determination to starve herself to death. The helplessness with which Buechner watched this daughter whom he passionately loved destroy herself propelled him, he tells us, into a "hell" of desperate fear.[21]

Finally the inevitable happened: Buechner's daughter collapsed and, near death, was hospitalized. Because he was some three thousand miles away at the time, Buechner was unable to run to her side "to protect her, to make her decisions, to manipulate events on her behalf"—to *make* her do the right thing.[22] Now, in the absence of a doting father who in the past had always pulled her chestnuts out of the fire, his daughter had to face the consequences of her decisions and behavior. "There was," recalls Buechner, "no one to shield her from those events and their consequences in all their inexorability."[23] Desperately as Buechner longed to save his daughter from herself, her doctors, nurses, and social workers managed to convince him that in this situation the best way to love her was to let her be, to enable her to make the choice for life on her own.

Happily, Buechner's daughter *did* choose life and eventually recovered. But the harrowing experience of her ordeal taught Buechner something about love. At the outset of his daughter's decline, he tells us, "the only way I knew to be a [loving] father was to take care of her…, to move heaven and earth if necessary to *make* her well." But in time he came to see the futility as well as the arrogance of such a position:

> I didn't have either the wisdom or the power to make her well. None of us has the power to change other human beings like that, and it would be a terrible power if we did, the power to violate the humanity of others even for their own good.[24]

Buechner finally understood that "the only way [his daughter] would ever be well again was if and when she *freely* chose to be." And the hard lesson for Buechner the parent, Buechner the shepherd, was that "the best I could do…was to stand back and give her that freedom even at the risk of her using it to choose for death instead of life."[25]

The soul-shaking experience of his daughter's illness taught Buechner that passionate love does not, cannot, stifle; parental love cannot force; shepherd love must not corner. Genuine love, unlike the "altruism" of good-eating, recognizes that since love is a gift freely given, it must be freely accepted by the beloved. To "lovingly" force someone, either out of reckless fear or blind passion, to do what is good for her is to treat her as a thing, a mindless, spiritless chess piece. Instead, love can only enable (in the sense of *aition*) others to be good by making itself available and being with them in their pain and weakness. This is a bitter pill to swallow for the parent, the spouse, or the shepherd—and even more for the good-eater—but it is one that nonetheless must be forced down. As Dorothy Day was wont to say, genuine love is sometimes a harsh and dreadful thing.

Buechner learned something else as well: Loving with passionate restraint in fact is an imitation of the way God loves us. The divine Lover spends himself in our service; his grace is always present to us, extended to us as a gift. But God will not, cannot, force the gift upon us any more than Buechner could force his gift on his daughter. In reflecting on what his experience revealed about the God who is Love, Buechner has this to say: "God loves in something like this way, I think. The power that created the universe and spun the dragonfly's wing and is beyond all other powers holds back, in love, from overpowering us." God, in other words, loves us too much to force our behavior. God is willing to take the terrible risk of losing us in order that we in turn might learn to love. This patience, this forbearance, this "passionate restraint and hush of God," is as essential a quality of genuine love as is profligacy.[26]

Not "love" on our own terms, but simply Love. Not the lawlike "good" decreed by our lust to dictate to others, but simply God's Good. Not abstract "altruism"—much less moral machismo—but the patience and compassion to meet and embrace concrete human beings where we meet them, in all our fragile vulnerability, in all their brokenness. Good-eating Herod, surrounded by his flow charts and statistics and plans for the Rational Life, knows nothing of this. The clamor of his own Godlust destroys any possibility of harkening to Love's tender hush. And that clamor is an echo of the tormented cries that well up from the abyss. For hell, the loss of the Good, is not to love.

Conclusion

Soul Food

Jesus said to them, "I am the bread of life; he
who comes to me shall not hunger, and he who
believes in me shall never thirst."

John 6:35

Herod...was tormented by lack of food.

Josephus

A Demonic Punch Line

Herod the Great ruled Judea for some four decades. His
reign was brilliant; neither his father before him nor sons after
him could match the sheer weight of his achievements or passions. When it came to diplomatic canniness, military skill,
architectural and engineering vision, courtly opulence, rapacity of appetite or personal brutality, Herod was unparalleled.

But this same Herod came to a horrible end. As we saw in
chapter 1, Josephus tells us he was maddened by unbearable

itching, stomach swelling, dropsy, gangrene, worms, and convulsions. Herod's entire body seems to have rotted out from under him, to have jumped the gun on postmortem decay. To top everything off, Herod also lost the ability to eat or drink, even though he retained his voracious appetite to the very end. His collapsing physical frame was simply unable to take in any more of what he had craved throughout his entire life. In a manner of speaking, Herod, the God-who-devours, died of starvation.

Josephus tells us that Herod's retainers whispered it about that the dying king's repellent collapse was a punishment from Yahweh. Perhaps. It depends on how one interprets divine retribution. But what's certain is that Herod's physical decay was a reflection of his spiritual rottenness. The worm of Godlust that for years gnawed at his vitals ultimately so destroyed his inner being that it had nothing left to turn to save his physical frame. This demonic tapeworm gave Herod no surcease from the need to gorge and to continue gorging. Even after it so sapped his energy that he could eat no longer, the worm clamored to be fed. So finally it devoured its host, the mighty Herod. Herod, whose Godlust obsessively drove him to absent God, was himself absented by his Godlust.

The Tempter has a sense of humor, and the joke is always at our expense.

Spiritual Wraithdom

The horror that overtook Herod is the inevitable terminus of unchecked Godlust, just as dissolution and decay are the outcomes of every untreated malady. The hunger to devour reality and thus become God corrodes our well-being because it is an assault against our true nature. Original Sin is not a weakness with which we're born, but an opportunistic infection that invades the soul and poisons our innate God-desire. Its toxic effects are insidious. They provoke a euphoric sense of power and authority even as they slowly sap our spiritual strength; they increase our appetite only to starve us to death. The soul-destroying virus of Godlust has been well described by Georges Bernanos as a "parasitic growth...forever threatening to stifle virility as well as intelligence. Impotent to create, it can only contaminate in the germ the frail promise of humanity; it is probably at the very source, the primal cause of all human blemishes."[1]

Bernanos's "promise of humanity" is the deification God wishes for us. It is the hope, whose foundation is laid by our deiform connectedness with the Creator, that we can grow into what humans are intended to be: souls shining with the presence of Christ, beings who are interpenetrated by and in turn interpenetrate divine Being. Our promise, our hope, our strength, our salvation, lies in becoming one in and with God just as Christ is (Jn 17:21). When that grace-filled possibility is "contaminated," as Bernanos says, we twist into stunted caricatures of what we might have been. We lose spiritual "virility" and become wraiths who frenziedly destroy our chances for the substance we so crave.

A page taken from the tantric Buddhist tradition grippingly illustrates the woeful nature of such a wraithlike existence. Tibetan Buddhists believe that the cosmos is populated by any number of entities. One of these is called the "hungry ghosts." As described by a Western commentator, hungry ghosts are "phantomlike creatures" who are "fusion[s] of rage and desire." This is because they're "tormented by unfulfilled cravings and insatiably demanding of impossible satisfactions." Their appearance is predictably grotesque: "withered limbs, grossly bloated bellies, and long, thin necks"—all reminiscent of Josephus's portrait of the dying Herod. Also like Herod, the hungry ghosts are utterly incapable of assuaging their appetites:

> [T]hese beings, while impossibly hungry and thirsty, cannot drink or eat without causing themselves terrible pain or indigestion. The very attempts to satisfy themselves cause more pain. Their long, thin throats are so narrow and raw that swallowing produces unbearable burning and irritation. Their bloated bellies are in turn unable to digest nourishment; attempts at gratification only yield a more intense hunger and craving.[2]

In the Tibetan worldview, hungry ghosts appear to be both actual entities and metaphors. As actual entities, they are the spirits of persons who have squandered their lives by restlessly demanding more than they could have and refusing to appreciate what was given them. Having fed on everything except what was good for them, they've retarded their spiritual growth and forever remain dwarfish and voracious. As metaphors, hungry ghosts stand for the illegitimate and unfulfillable longings that haunt and frustrate each human being. If the hold of these longings on our heart, mind, and spirit isn't broken, we anticipate in this life, just as Herod's body anticipated postmortem decay, the unhappy fate of those wraiths who inhabit the realm of the hungry ghosts: We become fusions of rage and desire, forever hungering, forever unfulfilled, forever raging.

Godlusters, haunted as they are by the metaphorical hungry ghosts of perverse longing, are well on their way to becoming actual hungry ghosts. Their lives are bounded by pain, first by the initial distress of their ontological anxiety and existential envy, then by the self-wounding inflicted by their futile attempts to usurp God's place. The divine food they scramble to devour isn't for them; their stomachs aren't strong enough to digest it, their tissues too finite to absorb it. Eating Truth, Beauty, and the Good won't palliate the sense of inadequacy wrought by fixation on deiformic separateness. Because it is a rebellion against God and because such rebellion is always doomed to end in forlorn frustration, the God-luster only succeeds in alienating herself even more from the Fullness she craves and perversely thinks she can claim for her own. She exiles herself deeper and deeper into the abyss of spiritual wraithdom where, like the Tibetan hungry ghosts, her vitals—her very substance—are eaten away by the tapeworm of Original Sin. The glorious deification that might have been hers collapses in the ruinous horror of demonization.

Breaking Bread

Wraiths, whether they're Buddhist hungry ghosts or Christian Godlusters, destroy themselves through their perverse appetites. They allow the natural and wholesome desire for God to explode into an unnatural and poisonous lust to be God. To compensate for their ontological anxiety and existential envy, they indulge in a hypertrophically arrogant sense of celestial entitlement, a peevish insistence on seeing God as the challenging Other who must be eaten and thereby absented.

Our separateness from God is a spiritual fact. But the proper response to it is not a manic gorging on Truth, Beauty, and the Good. As suggested in chapter 1, *partaking* of God, not *devouring* God, is the way to redress our forlorn anxiety. Partaking leads upwards to the glory of deification. Devouring hurtles us into the demonic pit.

Devouring is a deliberately solitary activity because it attempts to consume the entire universe and transform it into an extension of the eater's ego. The God-who-devours brooks no fellow feeders at reality's table. Everything on the menu must be his and his alone.

Partaking, on the other hand, is a way of responding to reality that celebrates the companionable presence of God and humans and embraces them as table companions in the holy feast of life. The Latin stresses the communality of partaking and companionship more emphatically than their English derivatives: *partake* comes from *particeps*, a "sharing in or taking part in," and *companionship* from *cum*="with" and *pan*="bread." Whereas devouring seeks to seize and monopolize, partaking is an act of grateful acceptance and generous sharing with boon companions (cf. Lk 19:5–6). The partaker "participates" with God and her fellow human beings in the recognition and celebration of Truth, Beauty, and Goodness. The devourer nudges both out of the way to claim everything for the imperial self. The partaker celebrates the presence of Christ in others and celebrates that presence in the intimacy of service and sharing (cf. Lk 7:12–14). The devourer reduces his relationship with persons to one of master and slave. The partaker celebrates dependency as a glorious reminder of her deiformic connectedness with God. The devourer abhors it as a noxious reminder of his deiformic separateness.

In short, the partaker realizes that there's plenty of bread at the divine repast to feed everyone, and she ceases her manic scrambling to be first in line. Divine grace falls like manna from heaven, and it falls every day, ceaselessly, bountifully. The loaves and fish offered us—God's Truth, God's Beauty, and God's Goodness—are as inexhaustible as they are enriching. The partaker also knows that the place of honor is at the bottom of the table rather than its head: The first are last and the last are first (Jn 13:2–5,12–17). Accordingly, her comportment at the table isn't one of hoggish gluttony, but rather one of service and sharing. Bread broken with others—companionship—is the only way to eat well.

And what is the bread that's passed around to all, that's communally eaten with love and gratitude and humility? John tells us (6:33, 41) that it is "the bread of God...which comes down from heaven, and gives life to the world." It is not bread *of* the world, although it is found *in* the world in signals of transcendence. It is the bread of Truth, Beauty, and Goodness, leavened by the risen Christ. To partake of it is to invite God into one's soul and one's soul into God so that the interpenetration spoken of by Saint Maximos, an interpenetration in which "the participant becomes like that in which he participates," comes to pass. Saint Catherine of Siena expressed the same insight in the thirteenth century when she wrote that Christ is our true food and table. "And we who eat at that table," she exulted, "become like the food, acting not for our own utility but for the honor of God and the salvation of neighbor."[3] For the partaker, all existence is a eucharistic opportunity, and every being in existence a table companion with whom to break and share the living bread.

The life-giving bread of God, the bread for which all God-desirers yearn (Jn 6:34): This is the manna of deification, this the proper food of *imago dei*. The grey bread of Godlust, the stale crust Herod the hungry ghost ceaselessly chews without satisfaction: This is the rust and ashes of demonization. We should remember Herod's fate. We should pray for him. But God forbid we follow in his steps.

Notes

Chapter One.

The chapter epigraphs are from Richard Crashaw's translation of Giambattista Marino's "*Sospetto d'Herode*" and C. S. Lewis's *That Hideous Strength*.

1. *Herod and the Kings*, in *Religious Drama 2: Mystery and Morality Plays*, ed. E. Martin Browne (New York: Meridian, 1958), p. 133.

2. Ibid., p. 134.

3. See St. Bonaventure, *The Mind's Road to God*, trans. George Boas (Indianapolis: Bobbs-Merrill, 1953) and Peter Berger, *A Rumor of Angels* (Garden City, N.Y.: Doubleday, 1969) and *A Far Glory* (New York: Anchor, 1993).

4. John Haught interestingly discusses a variety of signals of transcendence in *What Is God?* (Mahwah, N.J.: Paulist Press, 1986). See also Langdon Gilkey's discussion of "dimensions of sacrality and ultimacy" that permeate "secular" experience in *Naming the Whirlwind: The Renewal of God-Language* (Indianapolis: Bobbs-Merrill, 1969).

5. For an excellent discussion from a Thomistic perspective of Truth, Beauty, and Goodness as divine aspects, see Etienne Gilson,

The Elements of Christian Philosophy (New York: Mentor, 1960), pp. 149–78.

6. Pseudo-Dionysius the Areopagite, *The Divine Names and Mystical Theology*, trans. John D. Jones (Milwaukee: Marquette University Press, 1980), pp. 138–141.

7. Ilias the Presbyter, A *Gnomic Anthology*, in *The Philokalia*, ed. G. E. H. Palmer, Philip Sherrard, Kallistos Ware (London: Faber & Faber, 1984), vol. 3, p. 43.

8. The reference is to the famous line at the beginning of Augustine's *Confessions*, trans. Henry Chadwick (New York: Oxford University Press, 1992), p. 4: "Thou madest us toward [*ad te*, frequently mistranslated as "for"] Thyself, O God, and our hearts are restless until they repose in Thee."

9. Max Scheler, *Ressentiment*, trans. William W. Holdheim (New York: Schocken, 1972), p. 52.

10. For an insightful and now classic analysis of the "other," see Jean-Paul Sartre, *Being and Nothingness*, trans. Hazel E. Barnes (New York: Washington Square Press, 1966), part 3, chapter 1.

11. Ibid.

12. Robert Fabing, S.J., has published two recent reflections on the eucharistic partaking of God that are well worth consulting: *The Eucharist of Jesus* (Phoenix: North American Liturgy Resources, 1986) and *Real Food: A Spirituality of the Eucharist* (Mahwah, N.J.: Paulist Press, 1993).

13. James Frazier, *The New Golden Bough*, ed. Theodor H. Gaster (New York: Mentor, 1959), pp. 530–49.

14. Carol J. Adams, *The Sexual Politics of Meat: A Feminist-Vegetarian Critical Theory* (New York: Continuum, 1990), pp. 40–62.

15. See Ludwig Feuerbach, *The Essence of Christianity*, trans. George Eliot (New York: Harper, 1957) and Sigmund Freud, *The Future of an Illusion*, trans. James Strachey (New York: Norton, 1961).

16. Max Stirner, *The Ego and His Own*, trans. John Carroll (New York: Harper, 1974), p. 90.

17. Augustine, *On Free Choice of the Will*, trans. Anna S. Benjamin & L. H. Hackstaff (Indianapolis: Bobbs-Merrill, 1976), p. 8.

18. Thomas Aquinas also takes the I AM as highly significant. He interprets it as signifying the fact that God is existence/essence itself, is universal and absolute, and is eternal. Thomas goes on to agree with John Damascene, who says that the I AM "is the first of all names to be used of God…, for he comprehends all in himself, he has his existence as an ocean of being, infinite and unlimited." *Summa Theologica* (London: Blackfriars, 1964), Ia.xiii.xi.

19. John Milton, *Paradise Lost*, ed. Merritt Y. Hughes (New York: Odyssey Press, 1962), Book IX, line 658.

20. Ibid., lines 679–87.

21. Søren Kierkegaard, *Practice in Christianity*, trans. Edward V. & Edna H. Hong (Princeton: Princeton University Press, 1991), p. 26.

22. St. Maximos the Confessor, "Various Texts on Theology, the Divine Economy, and Virtue and Vice," in *The Philokalia*, ed. and trans. G. E. H. Palmer, Philip Sherrard, and Kallistos Ware (London: Faber & Faber, 1981), vol. 2, p. 239.

23. Plato, "Timaeus," in *Collected Dialogues*, ed. Edith Hamilton & Huntington Cairns; trans. Benjamin Jowett (Princeton: Princeton University Press, 1973), 29e–30a.

24. St. Mark the Ascetic, "Letter to Nicolas the Solitary," in *The*

Philokalia, ed. and trans. G. E. H. Palmer, Philip Sherrard, and Kallistos Ware (London: Faber & Faber, 1979), vol. 1, p. 155.

25. John Meyendorff, *Christ in Eastern Christian Thought* (Washington: Corpus Books, 1969), p. 164.

26. Tillich discusses the demonic in many works. For a typical treatment, see his *The Interpretation of History*, trans. N. A. Rasetzki & E. L. Talmey (New York: Scribners, 1936).

27. Daniel Day Williams, *The Demonic and the Divine*, ed. Stacy A. Evans (Minneapolis, Minn.: Fortress, 1990), pp. 6–14.

28. E. D. Klemke, "Living Without Appeal," in E. D. Klemke, ed., *The Meaning of Life* (New York: Oxford University Press, 1981), p. 171.

29. John Milton, *Paradise Lost*, Book X, lines 842–44.

30. Josephus, *The Jewish War*, trans. G. A. Williamson (New York: Penguin, 1981), p. 117.

31. Augustine, *On Free Choice of the Will*, p. 32.

Chapter Two.

The nonscriptural chapter epigraph is taken from one of Herod's speeches in the Wakefield mystery play *The Offering of the Magi*.

1. *The Offering of the Magi*, in Martial Rose, ed., *The Wakefield Mystery Plays* (New York: Anchor, 1963), p. 235.

2. Josephus recounts the sordid story of Herod's slaughter of Mariamme and his sons in *The Jewish War*, pp. 86–119. Josephus, who seems to have hero-worshipped Herod (or at least pretended to in front of his Roman patrons), predictably portrays Herod as the genuinely aggrieved party.

3. Friedrich Nietzsche, *The Will to Power*, trans. Walter Kaufmann (New York: Random House, 1967), p. 267.

4. Ibid., pp. 267, 298.

5. Peter Berger, *A Rumor of Angels*, pp. 34–60.

6. Friedrich Nietzsche, *The Will to Power*, p. 692.

7. Friedrich Nietzsche, *Beyond Good and Evil*, trans. Walter Kaufmann (New York: Random House, 1966), p. 14.

8. Friedrich Nietzsche, *The Will to Power*, pp. 526, 769.

9. Friedrich Nietzsche, "On Truth and Falsity in the Ultramoral Sense," in *Early Greek Philosophy and Other Essays*, trans. Maximillian A. Muegge (New York: Macmillan, 1911), p. 180.

10. Friedrich Nietzsche, *The Gay Science*, trans. Walter Kaufmann (New York: Random House, 1974), p. 280.

11. Friedrich Nietzsche, *The Will to Power*, pp. 267, 519.

12. Richard Rorty, *Contingency, Irony, and Solidarity* (Cambridge: Cambridge University Press, 1990), p. 5.

13. Ibid.

14. Ibid.

15. Richard Rorty, *Contingency, Irony, and Solidarity*, pp. 5, 8; see also "The World Well Lost," in *Consequences of Pragmatism* (Minneapolis: University of Minnesota Press, 1982).

16. Richard Rorty, *Contingency, Irony, and Solidarity*, p. 21.

17. Alvin Toffler, *Future Shock* (New York: Bantam, 1971).

18. Simone Weil, "Some Reflections on the Love of God," in *On*

Science, Necessity, and the Love of God, trans. Richard Rees (New York: Oxford University Press, 1968), p. 153.

19. Richard Rohr, *Job and the Mystery of Suffering: Spiritual Reflections* (New York: Crossroad, 1998), p. 163.

20. Søren Kierkegaard, *Practice in Christianity*, p. 205.

21. Augustine, *On Free Choice of the Will*, p. 65.

22. Ibid.

23. Karl Rahner, "The Hiddenness of God," in *Theological Investigations* XVI, trans. David Morland (London: Darton, Longman & Todd, 1979), p. 237.

24. I'm referring, of course, to Rudolf Otto's classic description of the experience of God as *mysterium tremendum et fascinans* in *The Idea of the Holy*, trans. John W. Harvey (London: Oxford University Press, 1923).

25. Ignatius, *Epistolae et Instructiones S. Ignatii* (Madrid, 1903–11), vol. 1, p. 626. Quoted by Hugo Rahner in *Ignatius the Theologian*, trans. Michael Berry (New York: Herder & Herder, 1968), p. 28.

26. Ignatius, *Spiritual Exercises*, trans. Anthony Mottola (Garden City, N.Y.: Doubleday, 1964), pp. 47–48.

27. Karl Rahner, "The Ignatian Mysticism of Joy in the World," in *Theological Investigations* III, trans. Karl-H. and Boniface Kruger (Baltimore: Helicon Press, 1967), p. 291.

28. Augustine, *Confessions*, Book 9, p. 172.

29. Augustine, *On Free Choice of the Will*, p. 143.

Chapter Three.

The nonscriptural chapter epigraph is from a speech by Herod in the Wakefield play, *The Offering of the Magi.*

   1. Josephus, *The Jewish War*, p. 81. For a magnificently illustrated account of the continuing archaeological excavation of Herod's city, see Kenneth G. Holum et al., *King Herod's Dream: Caesarea on the Sea* (New York: W. W. Norton, 1988).

   2. Augustine's discussions of beauty are voluminous. See, for example, *Confessions*, particularly Book 10, and *Of True Religion*, trans. J. H. S. Burleigh (Chicago: Henry Regnery, 1959), pp. 51–60. Dionysius the Areopagite discusses God's Beauty in Book 4 of *The Divine Names*. Hilary of Poitiers discusses *kosmos* in Book 1 of *The Trinity*, trans. E. W. Watson & L. Pullan in *Nicene and Post-Nicene Fathers*, Second Series, vol. 9 (Peabody, Mass.: Hendrickson, 1994). The Watson-Pullan translation is, unfortunately, sloppy; *kosmos* is frequently rendered as "order," even when the context clearly indicates that Hilary is focusing on divine and natural beauty. St. Francis's beauty-celebrating canticles can be found in many texts. One of the most accessible is Lawrence Cunningham ed, *Brother Francis: Writings by and about St. Francis of Assisi* (New York: Harper & Row, 1972). Two secondary sources worth consulting are Lynn White, "The Historical Roots of Our Ecological Crisis," *Science* 155 (1967): pp. 1203–7 and Edward A. Armstrong, *Saint Francis: Nature Mystic* (Berkeley: University of California Press, 1973). For citation of pertinent texts from Thomas Aquinas and Jonathan Edwards, see subsequent notes for this chapter. Recent works by theologians that explore Christian stewardship of nature include Richard Cartwright Austin, *Beauty of the Lord: Awakening the Senses* (Atlanta: John Knox Press, 1988); Thomas Berry, *The Dream of the Earth* (San Francisco: Sierra Club Books, 1988); Denis Edwards, *Jesus and the Cosmos* (Mahwah, N.J.: Paulist Press, 1991); Matthew Fox, *The Universe Is a Green Dragon* (Santa Fe: Bear & Co., 1983); John F. Haught, *The Promise of Nature:*

Ecology and Cosmic Purpose (Mahwah, N.J.: Paulist Press, 1993); and chapter 9 in Dorothee Soelle, *To Work and To Love: A Theology of Creation* (Philadelphia: Fortress, 1989). The titles mentioned here barely scratch the surface of the already vast and steadily growing literature of stewardship.

3. George Herbert Mead, *Movements of Thought in the Nineteenth Century*, ed. Merrit H. Moore (Chicago: University of Chicago Press, 1972), p. 261.

4. Friedrich Nietzsche, *Will to Power*, pp. 266, 328.

5. C. S. Lewis, *The Abolition of Man* (New York: Macmillan, 1947), pp. 13–15.

6. Francis Bacon, "The Refutation of Philosophies," ed. and trans. Benjamin Farrington, in *The Philosophy of Francis Bacon* (Chicago: University of Chicago Press, 1966), p. 130.

7. Francis Bacon, "De Dignitate et Augmentis Scientiarum," in *Works*, ed. James Spedding et al. (London: Longmans Green, 1870), vol. 4, pp. 296, 298.

8. Francis Bacon, "The Refutation of Philosophies, p. 130.

9. Francis Bacon, "The Masculine Birth of Time," in Farrington, *The Philosophy of Francis Bacon*, p. 62.

10. Martin Heidegger, "The Question Concerning Technology," in *Basic Writings*, ed. David Farrell Krell (San Francisco: Harper, 1993), pp. 314–15.

11. Ibid. p. 322.

12. Ibid., pp. 322–24.

13. Ibid., p. 330.

14. Yevgeny Zamyatin, We, trans. Gregory Zilboorg (New York: E. P. Dutton, 1959).

15. Martin Heidegger, "The Question Concerning Technology," pp. 321–22.

16. Ibid., p. 323.

17. This point is interestingly made by two recent commentators on contemporary science who derive quite opposite conclusions from it. Bryan Appleyard's Understanding the Present: Science and the Soul of Modern Man (New York: Doubleday, 1992), fears that science's totalizing tendencies are "spiritually corrosive" (p. 9). Carl Sagan's posthumous The Demon-Haunted World: Science as a Candle in the Dark (New York: Random House, 1995) applauds the totalization because science has the ability to "deliver the goods" which any "religion on the planet" would envy (p. 30).

18. Martin Heidegger, "The Question Concerning Technology," p. 333.

19. Ibid.

20. The Renaissance painter and chronicler Giorgio Vasari famously describes God as the First Artist in the opening paragraph of his Lives of the Artists, ed. and trans. George Bull (New York: Penguin, 1980).

21. Thomas Aquinas, Summa Theologica, 1a.xxxix.viii.

22. For three intriguing discussions of the relationship between God and beauty, see Richard Harries, Art and the Beauty of God: A Christian Understanding (London: Mowbray, 1993); Armand A. Maurer, C.S.B., About Beauty: A Thomistic Interpretation (Houston, Tex.: Center for Thomistic Studies, 1983); and Patrick Sherry, Spirit and Beauty (New York: Oxford University Press, 1992).

23. Jonathan Edwards, *The "Miscellanies,"* ed. Thomas A. Schafer (New Haven: Yale University Press, 1994), p. 384.

24. Jonathan Edwards, A *Dissertation Concerning the Nature of True Virtue* in *Works* (Edinburgh: Banner of Truth Trust, 1990), vol. 1, p. 125.

25. Jonathan Edwards, "The Mind," in *Scientific and Philosophical Writings,* ed. Wallace E. Anderson (New Haven: Yale University Press, 1980), p. 380.

26. Jonathan Edwards, "Beauty in the World," in *Scientific and Philosophical Writings,* pp. 305–6.

27. Jonathan Edwards, "The Mind," p. 380.

28. Jonathan Edwards, *The "Miscellanies,"* p. 279.

29. Ibid.

30. Ibid.

31. Martin Heidegger, "Building Dwelling Thinking," in *Basic Writings,* p. 363.

32. Jonathan Edwards, *The Nature of True Virtue,* p. 122.

33. Gerard Manley Hopkins, "God's Grandeur," in *Poems and Prose,* ed. W. H. Gardner (New York: Penguin, 1984), p. 27.

34. "Notebooks," 1872, in *Poems and Prose,* p. 127.

35. "Notebooks," 1871, in *Poems and Prose,* pp. 122, 123.

36. "Notebooks," 1870, in *Poems and Prose,* p. 119.

37. "Pied Beauty," in *Poems and Prose,* pp. 30–31.

38. Martin Heidegger, "Letter on Humanism," in *Basic Writings*, p. 245.

Chapter Four.

The nonscriptural chapter epigraph is from Herod's speech in W. H. Auden's "For the Time Being."

1. W. H. Auden, "For the Time Being," in *Collected Poems*, ed. Edward Mendelson (New York: Random House, 1991), p. 391.

2. Ibid., p. 392.

3. Ibid.

4. Ibid., p. 393.

5. Ibid., p. 394.

6. Ibid.

7. Machiavelli defends his "great man" thesis in *The Prince*, his manual for aspiring rulers written in the early sixteenth century. A typical example of his odious advice is as follows: "...in seizing a state one ought to consider all the injuries he will be obliged to inflict and then proceed to inflict them all at once so as to avoid a frequent repetition of such acts. Thus he will be able to create a feeling of security among his subjects, and by benefiting them, win their approval." *The Prince*, trans. Daniel Donno (New York: Bantam, 1981), p. 38. Nietzsche's discussions of the "great man," or *übermensch*, are scattered throughout his writings. Representative are these aphorisms from the section of *The Will to Power* entitled "The Masters of the Earth": "Each of us would like to be master over all men, if possible, and best of all God. This attitude must exist again." The "great man" is "colder, harder, less hesitating, and without fear of 'opinion'; he lacks the virtues that accompany respect and 'respectability';...he

wants no 'sympathetic' heart, but servants, tools; in his intercourse with men he is always intent on *making* something out of them." Love which is "divine"—that is, the "love" of the "great man,"—"despises…and reshapes and elevates the beloved." *The Will to Power*, pp. 503, 505, 506.

8. Søren Kierkegaard, *Fear and Trembling*, trans. Walter Lowrie (Princeton, N.J.: Princeton University Press, 1973), pp. 80, 79–80, 77.

9. Two excellent fictional illustrations of moral machismo's perverse appeal to Kierkegaard's teleological suspension of the ethical may be found in Fyodor Dostoevsky's *Crime and Punishment*, trans. Constance Garnett (New York: Dell, 1959) and Kurt Vonnegut's *Mother Night* (New York: Dell, 1974). In the first, the protagonist Raskolnikov puts himself above the moral demands he makes on everyone else by assuming for himself the right to kill an old pawnbroker whose existence he deems worthless. In the second, the "hero," Howard Campbell, Jr., argues that his collaboration with Nazis—behavior he would condemn as treason in others—is justified because performed for the sake of a "higher" purpose. Both men suffer from acute moral machismo: Convinced that their superior moral wisdom exempts them from "ordinary" ethical behavior, they suspend allegiance to it for the sake of a "greater" purpose, or *telos*.

10. It's instructive to note that Welles originally intended to call the screenplay (coauthored with Herman J. Mankiewicz) "The American" in order to underscore the chilling point that Kane's character is intended as a symbolic "everyman."

11. A more recent cinematic parable of spin-doctoring that makes a similar point is the 1997 satire, "Wag the Dog." There's no better and more disturbing recent film about political truth-eating.

12. Thomas Merton, *New Seeds of Contemplation* (New York: New Directions, 1972), p. 91.

13. Fyodor Dostoevsky, *The Brothers Karamazov*, trans. Constance Garnett (New York: Signet, 1960), p. 297; Georges Bernanos, *The Diary of a Country Priest*, trans. Pamela Morris (Garden City, N.Y.: Doubleday, 1974), p. 127.

14. Henri Nouwen brilliantly discusses the parental face of God's Love in his *The Return of the Prodigal Son: A Story of Homecoming* (New York: Doubleday, 1992), especially pp. 89–133.

15. The Song of Song's celebration of God's Love as spousal or romantic love has inspired centuries of commentary. The best certainly remains St. Bernard of Clairvaux's eleventh-century *Sermons on the Song of Songs*, in *The Works of Bernard of Clairvaux*, trans. Michael Casey et al. (Kalamazoo, Mich.: Cistercian Publications, 1969). Two recent commentaries, one Jewish and the other Christian, are also worth consulting: Jacob Neusner, *Israel's Love Affair with God: Song of Songs* (Valley Forge, Pa.: Trinity Press International, 1993) and Peter Kreeft, *Three Philosophies of Life* (San Francisco: Ignatius, 1989), especially pp. 97–140.

16. Dorothy Day, *On Pilgrimage: The Sixties* (New York: Curtis, 1972), p. 22.

17. William D. Miller, *All Is Grace* (New York: Doubleday, 1987), p. 105. Miller's book is a compendium of Day's writing on the spiritual life.

18. Ibid., p. 97.

19. Henri Nouwen, *Sabbatical Journey: The Diary of His Final Year* (New York: Crossroad, 1998), p. 14.

20. C. S. Lewis, "The Weight of Glory," in *The Weight of Glory and Other Addresses*, ed. Walter Hooper (New York: Collier, 1980), p. 19: "There are no *ordinary* people. You have never talked to a mere mortal....Next to the Blessed Sacrament itself, your neighbour is the holiest object presented to your senses. If he is your Christian neighbour,

he is holy in almost the same way, for in him also Christ *vere latitat*—the glorifier and the glorified, Glory Himself, is truly hidden."

21. Frederick Buechner, *Telling Secrets* (San Francisco: Harper, 1991), pp. 23, 25.

22. Ibid., p. 28.

23. Ibid.

24. Ibid., p. 26.

25. Ibid., p. 27.

26. Ibid., pp. 28, 29.

Conclusion.

The nonscriptural epigraph is from Josephus's *The Jewish War*.

1. Georges Bernanos, *The Diary of a Country Priest*, p. 98.

2. Mark Epstein, *Thoughts Without a Thinker: Psychotherapy from a Buddhist Perspective* (New York: Basic Books, 1995), p. 28.

3. Catherine of Siena, from a letter to her confessor, quoted in Caroline Walker Bynum, *Holy Feast and Holy Fast: The Religious Significance of Food to Medieval Women* (Berkeley: University of California Press, 1987), p. 245. Bynum's book is a brilliant reconstruction of the theology and spirituality of eating/partaking of Christ in thirteenth- and fourteenth-century European Christianity. I'm indebted to Karmen MacKendrick for introducing me to Bynum's work.